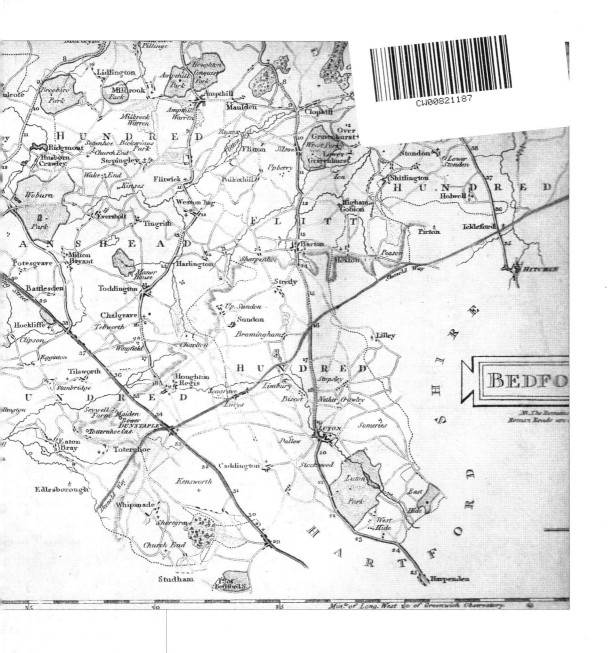

Details from Lyson's map of Bedfordshire (right) and Buckinghamshire (left) published in 1806. The Ouzel River is the common border for both maps.

LEIGHTON BUZZARD
AND
LINSLADE

A History

The High Street looking east towards the Market Cross and the Town Hall, one of the Piggott brothers' photographs, showing the centuries old Tuesday cattle market in full swing. It was taken around 1900.

LEIGHTON BUZZARD
AND
LINSLADE

A History

Paul Brown

A Leighton Buzzard and District Archaeological and Historical Society Project

PHILLIMORE

2008

Published by
PHILLIMORE & CO. LTD
Chichester, West Sussex, England
www.phillimore.co.uk
www.thehistorypress.co.uk

© Paul Brown, 2008

ISBN 978-1-86077-495-9

Printed and bound in Great Britain

Contents

LIST OF ILLUSTRATIONS

Frontispiece: High Street, Leighton, looking east, *c.*1900.

Illustration Acknowledgements

We are grateful to the following sources for use of their illustrations. All other pictures are the property of Leighton Buzzard and District Archaeological and Historical Society.

Bedfordshire and Luton Archives Service: Gurney collection; wills collection: 4, 8, 11, 23, 35, 50, 65, 76, 84, 98; John Bailey: 12, 61; Evelyn Baker: 29, 42; Terry Warburton: 37; Robert Richmond, *Leighton Buzzard and the Hamlets*: 55, 62, 66, 74; Mervyn Leah: 166; Wyvern Shipping: 83, 92, 100; Colin Holmes: Frontispiece, 70, 101, 107, 141, 143, 144, 145, 151, 158, 159; Tom Lawson: 102, 133, 134; Watson's Estate Agents: 125; Mrs E.R. Hammond: 146-7; Peter Tuthill: 162; Simon Videtta: 149.

All reasonable efforts have been made to find copyright holders for any illustrations used.

Acknowledgements

This history has been produced with the enthusiastic help of many people. It has been hard work, but fun, squeezing such a rich and varied history into one volume. So much new information has come to light in the course of writing it that those involved have already been inspired to enter new fields of research and discovery. Writing this volume would not have been possible at all without two special people: Maureen Brown and Barry Horne.

Maureen, my wife, with her knowledge and scholarship acquired by more than 30 years of research, has informed and guided the story as it has unfolded. Barry, with his technical skills, enthusiasm and knowledge of archaeology has been an invaluable partner.

Other committee members of Leighton Buzzard and District Archaeological and Historical Society (LBDAHS), Trudi Ball, Sue Baxter, Pauline Hey and Bernard Jones, have freely given their time, advice and expertise.

Many members of the society have allowed me to use their own research into local history, found illustrations and helped. Much of their work has previously been unpublished and I would particularly like to mention Andrew Date, Pat Griffin, Colin Holmes, Mike Jones, Ludovic McRae, Maggi Stannard and particularly Viv Willis for photographs and information. Thanks also to Jenny and Sue Bailey for allowing the use of their late father's drawings.

Others have helped with special skills, particularly Peter Gulland for drawing the original map of the area and Vanessa Hornby for the excellent illustrations of the plough team and the woolly mammoth.

Evelyn Baker generously allowed me to see her unpublished work on the dig at La Grava, and provided insights into Leighton's illustrious royal past.

Others have helped with such diverse problems as finding documents, writing down memories and opening churches to allow photographs of special features. Among them are John Deighton, Linda Eggleton, Mrs E.R. Hammond, Jack and Audrey Hillyer, Tom Lawson,

John Piggott, Peter Tuthill, Simon Videtta, Terry Warburton and Mike and Gene Ward.

Mr and Mrs Jack and Joan Horne have shown unfailing good humour while allowing their home to be invaded by history buffs.

The following institutions and their staff have been helpful with information and allowed us to reproduce their photographs and documents: Bedfordshire and Luton Archives Service, The Centre for Buckinghamshire Studies, Buckinghamshire Archaeological Society, Leighton Linslade Town Council and the Wyvern Shipping Company.

The royalties from this book are going to support the continuing efforts of the Leighton Buzzard and District Archaeological and Historical Society (www.LBDAHS.org.uk) to uncover and study the archaeology and history of the area and so inform current residents of their fascinating past.

Paul Brown
2008

I

Man and Mammoth

Woolly mammoths once roamed in what is now the Ouzel Valley. At different times as the climate changed, hippos, lions, horses and jackals were also native species. With these migrations came the first human hunters.

Animal bones and the stone tools, although few in number, are evidence of early Stone-Age peoples following the herds of wild animals. They came and disappeared again as warm periods were followed by ice ages. The warmth allowed the animals to advance and then the encroaching ice forced them to retreat again. During the ice ages massive glaciers sometimes came as far south as the Chilterns. After the last of these cold periods,

about 12,000 years ago, the animals, followed by man, gradually came back again. This was made easier because further north the ice cap was still miles thick and so widespread that massive quantities of water were locked in and the oceans were much lower as a result. The shallow area now filled by the English Channel was not a sea but a river valley allowing both animals and man to cross to Britain. At some point, about 8,500 years ago, the ice caps had melted sufficiently for Britain to become an island again.

1 Woolly Mammoth would have been common in the district at the time of the last Ice Age. The skeleton of one was found in Leighton Buzzard in the 19th century. It is now in the University Museum of Natural History at Oxford.

As the ice retreated from Bedfordshire for the final time the physical landscape would have been shaped much the same as today, with the current Ouzel Valley taking its present shape. Stone tools and bits of flint, carefully selected and shaped for different purposes, are evidence of the new wave of human immigrants who survived by hunting and trapping what must have been plentiful game. Some pieces of fashioned flint were stuck into wood to make spears. Other flakes were used as arrowheads and to act as knives. Sharp edged scrapers were needed to process skins for shelter and clothes. In 1972, at an excavation for sand extraction at Spring Close, Eggington, large numbers of these flint flakes hammered off larger flints were found by archaeologists on what would have been a dry hilltop, perfect for a hunter's camp. The area was surrounded by low-lying swampy land.

Recent discoveries, still being evaluated, provide additional evidence that this wave of migrants liked the Ouzel Valley so much they stayed. It seems that one of the earliest settlements of these Middle Stone-Age hunting tribes was in what are now the suburbs of Leighton Buzzard along Plantation Road. On a vantage point on a sandy bluff overlooking what are now the water meadows of the Ouzel, these new arrivals set up a seasonal camp. The concentration of stone tools found in the back gardens of homes overlooking the river encourages archaeologists to believe these items could not just have been dropped by passing hunters; it seems more likely that at least one tribe or family group stayed at this spot. The sandy soil would ensure the site was dry and relatively comfortable while local springs provided plentiful clean water. The good vantage point over the river, where herds of animals must have come to drink, was perfect for hunting, fishing and probably trapping water birds.

Identifying these sites is rare and exact dating is impossible, but primitive stone tools found in Leighton Buzzard used by these hunting people are believed to be more than 6,000 years old. Archaeologists label this era

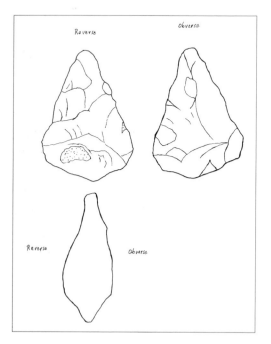

2   A drawing of a Palaeolithic Axe found in the area of Bossington during the 19th century. Its exact find spot is not known but the axe is now in the Ashmolean Museum, Oxford. The length is about 3½ inches and it seems to have been a general-purpose tool used by the Old Stone Age people. It pre-dates the last glaciation.

3   *These stone tools called microliths date from the Mesolithic period, after the last Ice Age, when the Ouzel Valley area was being recolonised by people. They were found in 2008 at Woodland Avenue, Leighton Buzzard. They probably mark a place where early hunters camped, watching for animals feeding and drinking in the river valley.*

Mesolithic – the period from when man first re-colonised Britain after the ice retreated to around 6,000 years ago. In one sense this is a completely arbitrary date, because over the centuries hunters must have been gradually developing more sophisticated tools, weapons and hunting methods.

Archaeologists believe, however, that changes in Stone-Age technology and the adoption of farming marked a definite change, and the next period in man's development is therefore known as the Neolithic. Some archaeologists believe that new waves of migrants from the continent joined the original inhabitants during this period and brought with them some newer technology and farm animals like cows, sheep and goats.

As with the rest of history, most changes evolved rather than happened overnight. Even so it is clear that lifestyles certainly changed during this period, with Neolithic people becoming more settled and taking up farming. Diets in the Mesolithic period included a lot of fish, nuts and berries but changed relatively suddenly to meat and grains, as farming appears to have become the main source of food.

Archaeological finds in Leighton show that Neolithic people were active in the area at the same time as Stonehenge was constructed. It seems likely that during the whole Neolithic

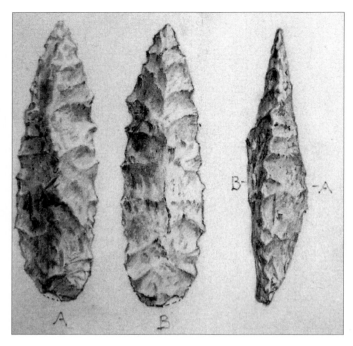

4 *Three views of an arrowhead found by local historian Frederick Gurney in Linslade in 1921. It is 2 inches long and was found with a number of others, but unfortunately the exact location was not recorded. It probably dates from the Neolithic or New Stone Age.*

to the Ouzel, some pottery believed to be Neolithic was also found – but there may be much more to discover. Excavations for the Linslade and Stoke Hammond bypass, for example, found 86 pieces of flint fashioned by man and ascribed to this period, although they were scattered rather than found in one place, which would have indicated a settlement.

The professional archaeologists who investigated the soils below the bypass and many amateurs from current and previous eras have found more evidence of the next phase of man's development in the Leighton area – the Bronze Age. Bronze represents a great leap forward in human technology. The knowledge of how to smelt bronze spread to Britain from the continent 2,000 years before the Romans arrived, showing that from the earliest times there was trade, or at least some links, between these islands and the continent.

Stone tools were still much in use but the ability to smelt a bronze alloy, made up of two-thirds copper and one-third tin, was a dramatic step. Mining had occurred before, for example for flints in Norfolk, but the ore to produce such high status implements must have created mining industries and important trade routes across Britain.

The oldest man-made constructions still visible in Leighton Buzzard are from this era.

period of around 2,000 years the Ouzel Valley supported family groups. Along the chalk downlands of the Chilterns at Puddlehill, Dunstable and Totternhoe pits have been dug, although for what purpose is unknown. Some burials and pottery from the period have also been found – this is only five miles from Leighton Buzzard. Together with finds of stone axes and earthworks at Maiden Bower, north of Dunstable, which may have been a causewayed enclosure on the hilltop, it seems that at least those areas had settled populations.

In Leighton Buzzard itself axe heads, flint blades and arrowheads have been picked up in quarries and in Page's Park. During the extensive archaeological dig at Grovebury, next

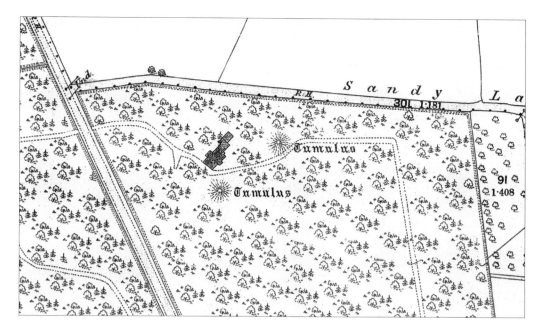

5 *Two Bronze-Age barrows or burial mounds known as 'The Knolls' as represented on the Ordnance Survey map of 1890. They are to the east of Plantation Road. The house is The Knolls as built by the Bassett family.*

Two Bronze-Age ditched barrows, or grave mounds, are now, incongruously, partly in the back garden of a 1970s housing development at Redwood Glade, off Plantation Road. This is very close to the newly discovered Mesolithic site mentioned earlier. Both overlook the Ouzel Valley.

These two barrows were relatively undisturbed, standing on unploughed heathland until the 19th century. Although dug into by curious Victorian antiquarians who found nothing, they were left alone until around 120 years ago when they were incorporated into the grounds of a large country house called The Knolls, which took its name from these two humps. The mounds have been mutilated and damaged subsequently, not least by subdividing some of The Knolls grounds into private gardens. A Bronze-Age incense cup, found nearby and believed to come from one of these mounds, is now in the Bedford Museum.

6 *One of the burial mounds as it looked in 2008 in the back garden of a new home built in the grounds of The Knolls. The ancient feature is almost lost.*

7 *A small 'incense cup' believed to have been found near The Knolls. It appears to be Bronze-Age in date. It is 3½ inches in diameter and 1½ inches high. It is in Bedford Museum.*

Local antiquarians have recorded other Bronze-Age barrows, one near the already mentioned Grovebury site to the south of Leighton. The top of this mound was sufficiently high to be used as a suitable site for a windmill for the medieval priory near the site, which is the subject of a subsequent chapter. Both the windmill base and the burial mound disappeared when the area was dug up for a sandpit.

Another fascinating area of humps and bumps that might have yielded much information about our ancestors was on the other side of town between the ancient Linslade Wood, also known locally as Bluebell Wood, and the boundary of the parish. Exactly how many man-made mounds there were is unknown, although the Anglo-Saxon charter of A.D. 966 mentions a number of 'hlaws' which is translated as 'burial mounds'. These mounds survived for so long because the area was unused heathland, that is until the railway came along in 1837 and the largest of the barrows was apparently levelled to provide ballast for the railway embankment. Subsequently the rest of the barrows were levelled and ploughed. Their age, size and possible contents remain a mystery.

Other finds in the district from this period include a food vessel and an urn so it is clear that the Ouzel Valley continued to be inhabited.

This account of early signs of man in the Leighton Linslade area has already travelled through more than 9,000 years of history. The available evidence of stone tools, burial mounds and the first rudimentary pottery can provide only tantalising evidence of occupation by our ancestors.

8 *This is a watercolour by Henry Dryden in 1843 of a Bronze-Age dagger found in 1837 during railway construction work at Jackdaw Hill, Linslade.*

9 *A modern reconstruction of an Iron-Age roundhouse at the Chiltern Open Air Museum. Houses similar in appearance to this would have been lived in for over a thousand years probably along ancient trackways through Bedfordshire and Buckinghamshire.*

The next phase, which again begins with another technological leap forward, this time the smelting of iron into more durable tools and weapons, sees Leighton Buzzard as part of a tribal Britain which is also an evolving farming and trading society.

Like previous archaeological periods, the Iron Age has fuzzy edges. Some say that it starts around 3,000 years ago, but others do not believe production of iron took place in Britain for another 300 to 500 years after that, around 2,500 years ago. Either way, the Roman era began with the successful invasion of Britain in A.D. 43 – so it lasted between 500 to 1,000 years in total. Unlike the earlier periods, it is clear that fixed settlements existed for significant lengths of time at different locations around Leighton Buzzard.

Recent excavations for the bypass on the high ground between Wing, Soulbury and Leighton Buzzard revealed there was an Iron-Age settlement where people lived in a number of round houses. There were no defensive earthworks but plenty of domestic pottery and remains of animal bones that

showed the people kept cattle, sheep and goats. There were also the remains of horses but no trace at all of pigs.

The archaeologists piecing together other discoveries from around the Ouzel Valley say that there is increasing evidence of quite dense settlements during the Iron Age. The bypass dig also revealed hearths or kilns for non-ferrous metal smelting in the settlement above modern Linslade. This could be for the continuing working of bronze or for other metal objects like jewellery. There is no evidence of arable farming and archaeologists believe, therefore, that the local people traded animals or other goods for grain. Absence of iron working shows that either they did not have the technology, or that it was a specialised trade which would have required trading goods in order to obtain iron objects.

Another favoured spot for our Iron-Age ancestors was Billington Hill, again overlooking the current town and the river valley. This time, however, the crest of the hill was surrounded by an earthwork, a large

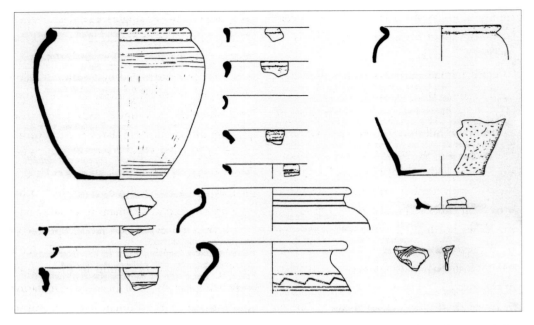

10 *Drawings of late Iron-Age pottery from Stone Lane, Heath and Reach. This is typical everyday ware which would have been used to store and cook food in Iron-Age roundhouses.*

rampart and ditch. This area was occupied for 1,000 years judging by the large quantities of pottery from different periods recovered. Skulls and bones were also found at the site. It is not clear whether this earthwork was intended to be a defensible position or to mark the boundaries of a settlement. Sadly, the earthwork was bulldozed in 1959.

A similar story of destruction involves an area called the Craddocks, now the site of the Leighton Buzzard Golf Course. A hilltop area of 30 acres was surrounded by a bank and ditch which experts believe is Iron-Age or perhaps even earlier. It is similar to the Maiden Bower site but the purpose and use of both sites is uncertain. Sadly, so much of this site has been altered and destroyed that unless there are some lucky finds, perhaps when digging a new bunker, the mystery of

the Craddocks will remain unsolved. Apart from these three sites there is evidence of occupation at other places on higher ground, again from Eggington, which seems to have been continuously occupied, or at least re-occupied by successive waves of people.

Throughout the Iron-Age period tribes all over Britain were building hill forts. The nearest one, which even the untrained eye can spot immediately, is at Ivinghoe Beacon, five miles to the south of Leighton Buzzard. It is in the care of the National Trust so is easy to visit and walk over. It has recently been dated as 3,000 years old – local people obviously felt the need to construct formidable earthworks by this time. Again, earthworks on this scale could only have been achieved by good organisation and a lot of people. Whether these earthworks were always for defence or simply as a way for a local chief to make a statement about his power and status is not certain.

Until Julius Caesar first visited Britain in 55 B.C. there is no description of what local tribes were like, although it is clear from the evidence of hill forts elsewhere that some felt the need for impregnable strongholds, since many had a series of banks and ditches topped with timber palisades. Caesar ran into formidable resistance and it seems that the tribes north of the Thames, which had been previously fighting each other to gain territory, united against the common threat of the invader.

It was nearly 100 years before the Romans invaded again, this time to stay. Meanwhile the local tribes had amalgamated and become a single tribe called the Catuvellauni. Sometime after Caesar's original attacks, they

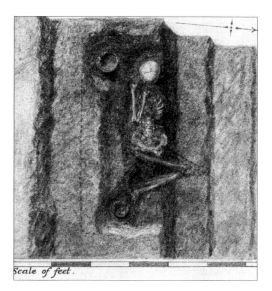

11 *An Iron-Age burial found at Eggington. It is unusual to find any burials from this period but it is particularly rare because normally chemicals in sand destroy bone.*

were united under a single leader Tasciovanus. He seems to have minted coins in St Albans, judging by the number found depicting his head. He was succeeded by a series of rulers who, by the time of this invasion, were trading with the Roman Empire, exporting cattle, grain, hunting dogs and slaves and importing wine and such luxury goods as silver cups, bronze serving dishes and even glass. It may be that it was the wealth of the British tribes that encouraged the Romans to invade again.

There is no evidence that the people of Leighton Buzzard took part in this trade aside from two coins found in the district, which appear to have been in circulation and lost before the Roman invasion. Either way, those living in this part of Bedfordshire would have been members, or under the control, of this tribe.

Although the Romans faced fierce resistance when they invaded Britain in A.D. 43, the main battlegrounds were in Kent and during the crossing of the Thames. By the time the Romans had reached what is now the Bedfordshire/Buckinghamshire border, the local chiefs had either been killed or had already made peace.

What effect this change of rulers had on daily life is impossible to tell. Archaeological finds in the district during the Roman period show that there was some occupation. Various Roman coins have been found, for example three in Leighton's All Saints' churchyard, with widely different dates suggesting they were lost as much as 100 years apart. Roman burials have also been uncovered at Grovebury, Tiddingford Hill in Linslade and Vandyke Road.

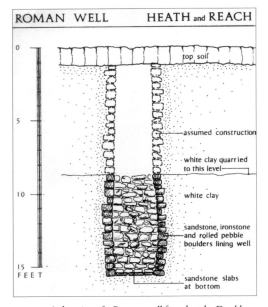

ROMAN WELL   HEATH and REACH

0

top soil

5

assumed construction

white clay quarried
to this level

10

white clay

sandstone, ironstone
and rolled pebble
boulders lining well

15
FEET

sandstone slabs
at bottom

12   *A drawing of a Roman well found at the Double Arches Pit during surface stripping operations. Two complete Roman pots were recovered, one of which had been repaired by lead plugs. In the area other finds of Roman date were destroyed during sand extraction and it is possible that a large Roman complex was lost.*

13   *The concave shape of this object tells us that it is the top stone of a Roman quern. The stone, found in Double Arches sand quarry, Heath and Reach, would have pivoted on a rod through the centre and turned by a handle in the hole in the side. Many hours would have been spent grinding wheat for flour to make bread.*

Despite the proximity of Watling Street, on the same line as the current A5 through Hockliffe, which must have been busy with soldiers and trade, there is no evidence of a Roman fort or larger settlement close to Leighton Buzzard. It seems that the local people carried on living in the same places as before. Favoured sites from previous eras such as Eggington, where a mile-long stretch on the ridge has had Romano-British pottery found along its length, were in continuous occupation. At Billington locals were also using Roman pottery. The Stoke Hammond and Linslade bypass construction shows that during the three centuries of Roman occupation farming continued on the hills.

Close to the A5 at Heath and Reach there may have been a Roman farm or villa. There was, for example, a Roman well uncovered during sand quarrying at Double Arches Quarry in the village. Close to Overend Green Farm considerable quantities of Roman pottery, tile, animal bones, a floor area and building remains have been found. Sadly no detailed excavation was carried out so the dimensions and importance of the Roman site was never documented.

Although the Roman era is perhaps the best-known and documented period of ancient British history it seems to have left less of a mark on Leighton Buzzard than the centuries immediately following. After the Romans departed new invaders arrived. The area between the A5 and the Ouzel became a royal estate and a ford in the river earned a place in national history.

2

The English Border Country

When the Romans abandoned Britain to home rule in A.D. 410 there is plenty of archaeological evidence that the southern half of the country was a prosperous and well-ordered society with affluent cities fed from a well-tended countryside dotted with luxurious villas. The Britons, who had long been declared Roman citizens, were left to fend for themselves. The legions were recalled to defend the crumbling empire in Europe from attacks by barbarians from the north and east.

This period is often referred to as the Dark Ages, but this reflects more our lack of written records of the time and so our knowledge of them, rather than a sudden sinister turn of events. At first, at least in the Chiltern area and the Ouzel Valley, the evidence is that life among what are called the Romano-British continued much as it had before. The widespread use of money that had been in circulation in the form of pay for the legions disappeared and some of the villas were abandoned by their owners, although they continued to be used as farm buildings,

workshops and for storage. Refinements like bathhouses and central heating also fell into disuse but the estates and their fields were continuously farmed.

The administration for the Ouzel Valley was based in Verulamium, modern St Albans, a walled city covering 200 acres with a population of around 15,000. Communications were good along the network of military roads and although it was a long way from the sea the locals must have been aware of raids from waterborne Germanic tribes, which troubled East Anglia and threatened trade.

There was a chain of villas along the Chilterns and the population of the country had grown considerably during the relatively peaceful Roman period of nearly 400 years. The weather had been particularly good and warm for most of the period and crops were grown for export. Britain was self-sufficient in wine. The country's population was believed to be around five million, a figure that dropped dramatically in the coming centuries. That high point was not reached again for another 900 years, during another climatically warm period.

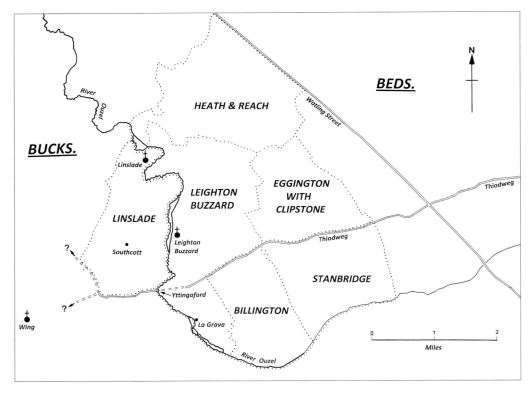

14 *The royal estate of Leighton between the River Ouzel and Watling Street, now the A5, showing the boundaries of the individual hamlets. These later became the parish boundaries. The major prehistoric route, Thiodweg, cut through the estate and its importance is marked by the fact that the parish boundaries ran along the road. Linslade's southern boundary on the other side of the Ouzel also runs along this road, which crosses the river at the ancient ford of Yttingaford. Thiodweg, in Anglo-Saxon 'the people's way', is also written Thedeway, The Edeway, and sometimes Saltway or Portway.*

When the legions left there was considerable organisation and manpower remaining. This was enough to provide some self-defence and, in addition, the affluent Britons hired mercenaries from the continent to defend them from the barbarian threat.

At any rate a continental visitor, St Germanus, in one of the last Roman references to the British, recalls that when he visited St Albans in A.D. 429 conditions were normal. Archaeological evidence tends to support the view that life in the city remained on the Roman pattern with a new water main being laid as late as A.D. 460, half a century after the legions departed.

Saxon invaders kept pushing inland, however, and took control of Kent, Sussex and much of East Anglia. But the British fought back, and under a king or chief who has come down to us as the fabled King Arthur, there was a resounding victory over the Saxons at Mount Badon in about A.D. 500. Such is the scant information about the period that no one has pinned down the whereabouts of Mount Badon or the lineage of the king who won this decisive battle. What is clear, however, is that this was a significant set-back for the Saxons, and large numbers were reported to have returned to the continent. The British continued to rule large parts of the country.

It is believed that the area that is now Leighton Buzzard remained under the control of the British, but at about this time there is the first evidence of a Saxon presence – a very early Saxon cemetery. At the same time the line of former Roman estates along the Chilterns and the Icknield Way continued farming under British control. Historians believe that these early Leighton Buzzard Saxons may have either been allowed to live and farm in the area as part of a complex peace deal following the Mount Badon battle or were part of the original mercenary force that had remained loyal to the British. In any event, they appear for at least two generations to have lived in peace on the British side of the border – which was apparently at Bedford. This settlement had been fortified to guard the strategic river crossing.

Bede, a Northumbrian monk writing in A.D. 730, 200 years after these events, said the Saxons that invaded East Anglia came from Old Saxony, the Angles from Angeln, now East Schleswig, and the Jutes from Jutland. Although clearly these people came from different tribes and brought with them their own heathen customs and gods, they also eventually integrated into one society.

So, 160 years after the Romans left, Britain was divided into two warring races: the British and the invaders, known generally as the Anglo-Saxons.

The peace after the battle of Mount Badon lasted approximately seventy years. According to the Anglo-Saxon Chronicles there was apparently another decisive battle at around A.D. 571 at Bedford where this time the Saxons won. They overran the British who were pushed back to Wales and the West Country, some even fleeing to Brittany and northern Spain. The Anglo-Saxons broke out from East Anglia, Kent and Sussex and moved west and north. They took most of what we now call England and became the English.

Exactly what sparked the successful overthrow of the British who had been so successful under their then leader, 'King Arthur', is not certain, but two events are significant. The first was a huge volcanic eruption somewhere on the other side of the world that caused A.D. 535 to be 'a year without a summer' and brought widespread famine. Examination of tree rings show almost no growth for four years and the adverse conditions must have severely disrupted crops.

A second disaster was the Yellow Plague, otherwise believed to be Bubonic Plague, that ravaged and further weakened the remaining Roman Empire. This was recorded as beginning around A.D. 540 and reached Britain about ten years later, having spread from southern Europe. Many thousands died during this outbreak. Until recently the potential political significance of these catastrophes has been poorly understood. Such climatic events could have damaged the harvests for more than one year and, coupled with the plague that followed, considerably weakened organised society and its ability to raise sufficient fighting men to defend their territories. The Anglo-Saxon Chronicles say that famines were regular occurrences because of deteriorating weather across Europe and subsequent poor harvests. The population fluctuated and fell as a result.

Although the date of A.D. 571 for the decisive victory of the Saxons over the British might not be exactly correct, it is clear from the archaeological evidence that the Saxons were in control from around that time.

There was a Saxon cemetery in Leighton Buzzard before this date and so logically there was a settlement, probably on the banks of the Ouzel where the current town stands. It is also clear from a seventh-century hall house found at Grovebury, two miles south of the town, that this area was important for early Saxon settlement. Exactly who lived at

Grovebury and their status is not known, but archaeologists found carefully marked out plots of land surrounded by ditches on the site indicating both sophisticated organisation and measuring techniques. Saxon graveyards found north of Leighton Buzzard show that at least some of the area where Leighton Buzzard now stands was settled by these new immigrants. Anglo-Saxon cemeteries with grave goods from this period were uncovered as early as the 1880s in sand diggings. As more quarries were opened in the 1930s, graves from slightly later Saxon periods were also found.

One of the old field names where the first graves were found just to the north of the town was Deadman's Slade, a clear indication that the existence of the ancient pagan graveyard was known well before

15 *String of 15 polychrome glass beads, which sand quarry owner Joseph Arnold took to historian Frederick Gurney in 1931, displayed among other Anglo-Saxon finds at Luton Museum. The beads alerted Gurney to the two Anglo-Saxon cemeteries at Chamberlain's Barn, north of Leighton town. They have been dated to the early seventh century and are from a grave in the earlier of the two cemeteries.*

16 *A fragment of a composite disc brooch found in a grave in the second and later cemetery at Chamberlain's Barn. Each of the bosses has a central garnet, the outer bosses each have a surround of flat garnets. The two surviving plates are of decorated gold sheet. This cemetery seems to date from the mid-seventh century and is probably Christian but the presence of grave goods shows the relatives of the dead were not yet willing to give up all of their pagan beliefs.*

date and was probably from the wave of Saxons that arrived after the Britons had been driven from the region. It contained grave goods typical of a pagan Saxon culture. A third, later, cemetery was close by with few grave goods but some other interesting features. Here the burials were in orderly rows and faced east-west. Archaeologists believe that the first two cemeteries were from the pagan Saxon period and the third dates from when the Saxons converted to Christianity. This 'conversion' ties in with the battle for supremacy between the Saxon kingdoms of Wessex and Mercia. The Leighton Buzzard area changed hands more than once but became part of Christian Mercia around A.D. 650.

the Victorians 'discovered' it. The second graveyard, at Chamberlain's Barn, only a short distance away, was of a slightly later

Evidence of tangible Christianity in this area comes from excavations at the ancient church in Wing, which was founded about this time, around the end of the seventh century. This church was probably built

17 *Two pins, which were originally linked by a chain, from a grave in the same cemetery at Chamberlain's Barn as the disc brooch. They are silver with flat garnets.*

18 *This collection of jewellery was found in a single grave in the second cemetery. Originally there were two linked silver pins with garnets. Below that there are seven silver wire rings (there had been 10) that were strung together with the five beads. At the bottom is a pendant made of a sheet of silver.*

on a pagan site and the substantial stone minster church, the home of missionary preachers, was constructed in a grand manner to emphasise the dominance of the new religion. The remains of this first church are incorporated into the existing building and the crypt under the church is believed to be a rare survival from the original minster. It is likely that there was a small daughter church or a preaching cross in the Saxon settlement at Leighton Buzzard only three miles away and that the local inhabitants embraced the new religion of their rulers.

One of the edicts of the new religion was that Christians should abandon old pagan graveyards and start new Christian ones. This would account for there being two graveyards at Chamberlain's Barn for the same settlement, the latter with graves orientated east-west in the Christian tradition. Old habits and superstitions are hard to eradicate, however, which would explain why some graves still contained grave goods, although fewer than in the pagan graveyard. Missionaries were still trying to prevent families burying goods with their relatives in Christian graves a century later.

Perhaps the most interesting feature of the Leighton Buzzard area at this time was the east-west roadway known as 'Thiodweg'. Translated from the Anglo-Saxon it means 'the public, or people's, highway'. In a large variety of documents through the centuries it is also called 'Thedeway', 'Ede Way' and

19   *The church of All Saints at Wing, showing the ancient apse at the eastern end. A rare survival is the Anglo-Saxon arched decoration on the stonework. The picture shows the original windows lighting the crypt below. This is one of very few remaining Anglo-Saxon buildings in England and when built must have been a beacon of early Christianity.*

20 *The crypt under the apse at Wing church, the earliest part of the building. It is believed to have been built before A.D. 700 and would have housed precious Christian relics. Shown here is the entry from the church, now blocked, which would have given access to the crypt for the congregation to process around the relics.*

This ancient road crossed the River Ouzel, then a much larger river, at Yttingaford. This name lingers on in Tiddenfoot, the local sports centre and nearby park. The old ford still exists several hundred feet away on the other side of the canal. Although now cut off from any roadway or footpath it can be viewed from the southern bypass, where there is a bridge over the canal. The ford is near a point where the old boundaries of Bedfordshire and Buckinghamshire met, along with the parishes of Leighton Buzzard, Linslade and Grove. Its importance as a boundary was made clear by the Anglo-Saxon Chronicles, which name Yttingaford in A.D. 906 as being the site of Edward the Elder's peacemaking with the Danes.

Our history moves forward 200 years here, to a period when Leighton Buzzard was again on the front line between two peoples and cultures. This time it was the Anglo-Saxons who were fighting a rearguard action against invaders, the Danes who, like the Saxons before, had at first raided and then decided to settle in England and pushed the local people back from settlements in East Anglia towards the west.

As with the Saxons and Britons 400 years before, the tides of war ebbed backwards and forwards across the Chiltern region and put the Ouzel Valley and its settlements in the front line.

Edward, the son of Alfred the Great, had faced a challenge for the throne from a cousin who had allied with the Danes in the hope of using their army along with his followers to further his claim to the throne. Edward's cousin was killed in battle and the subsequent

sometimes the 'Saltway' but it is the same route. This road is hardly known compared with the much more famous and still well-trodden route, the Icknield Way, which runs along the Chilterns five miles to the south. Both probably pre-date the Roman period and may have prehistoric origins. The importance of this local ancient trackway through many centuries is clear. The route of the road still forms the parish boundaries of Eggington with Stanbridge and Billington with Leighton Buzzard. The road remained in use through the medieval period until a bridge was built in Leighton Buzzard.

21 *Yttingaford, which continued in use until the 20th century as a river crossing for huntsmen, was where the Thiodweg crossed the Ouzel. It was here that the Wessex king, Edward the Elder, and Guthrum, the Danish warlord, met to declare a peace treaty in 906. At this time the Ouzel marked the boundary between Wessex and the Danelaw, the area controlled by the Viking invaders.*

22 *The comb in the centre of this picture was found in an archaeological dig in Eggington, one of the longest continually inhabited sites in the district. The village green borders the ancient Thiodweg. The comb is made of a number of plates of worked bone riveted together.*

terms of the peace were dictated by Edward at Yttingaford, according to the Anglo-Saxon Chronicles. The river, or possibly nearby Watling Street, formed the boundary between the Anglo-Saxons and the Danes. Excavations at Grovebury suggest that the Danes occupied this site at around this time so it is more likely that the Ouzel was the border between the two peoples.

This early mention of Yttingaford and the Ouzel as a boundary is repeated in a charter for Linslade of A.D. 966. This remarkable document, exactly 100 years earlier than the Norman invasion, gives the first descriptions of the landscape round Linslade. The purpose of describing the trees, streams and fields at the time is to record the boundaries of the Saxon estate. It is not clear to historians whether at the time of this charter the boundaries between Saxon and Dane domination had changed. While at a national level there continued to be battles over who ruled England, distinctions between races at local level might have lessened. One hundred and ten years after the peace at Yttingaford, England had a Danish King, Cnut. He ruled between 1017-36. By then, intermarriage between various royal houses made succession complicated. In Linslade and Leighton past allegiances between Saxon and Dane might have been redundant.

The A.D. 966 charter's purpose was to record the boundaries of the estate of Linslade, which had been given as a gift by one member of the royal family to another. Many estates were owned by the ruling classes who owed allegiance to the king. They raised fighting men for the army and in return kept valuable lands for growing crops and keeping animals.

Linslade was a small estate with a village of the same name where St Mary's Church now stands. This charter is the first known mention of the name. The estate was given to a lady called Aelfgyfu. She had once been Queen of England and had apparently been given the estate along with Wing and a large number of other lands including Berkhamsted and Hatfield. At the time of her death she was described as an illustrious woman who had commended herself to the prayers of the community by gift of alms. However, as a young woman she was involved in a royal scandal. On 27 January 956, according to the Anglo-Saxon Chronicles, the young Saxon King Edwy had been anointed and crowned king. He left the feast after the ceremony to enjoy the company of his intended bride, Aelfgyfu, and her mother. The nobles felt insulted by this action and Abbot Dunstan went to fetch him back only to discover the King amusing himself with both ladies, his crown left lying on the ground. It was claimed that the King was 'repeatedly wallowing between the two of them in an evil fashion, as if in a vile sty'.

Edwy subsequently married Aelfgyfu although closely related to her, according to the Chronicles, and the union was frowned upon by the church. Edwy's reign only lasted four years and he met his death in suspicious circumstances.

Aelfgyfu was a survivor and seems to have supported the new King Edgar immediately and turned to the church for guidance and help. Linslade was among the gifts the new King gave her, presumably partly in gratitude

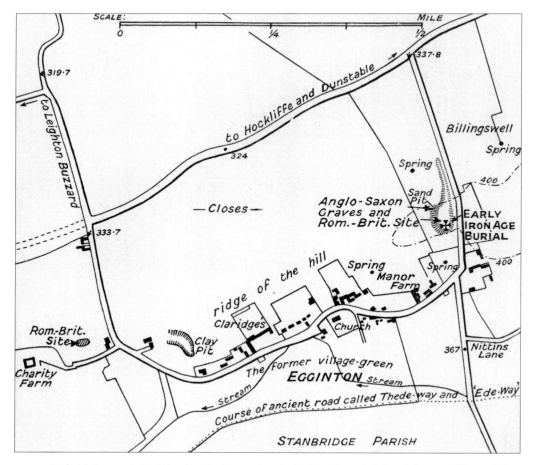

23 *Frederick Gurney, the local historian who discovered much of Leighton's past including the location of Yttingaford, drew this map to show Iron-Age, Roman and Anglo-Saxon sites he found in his home village of Eggington. He lived at a house called Claridges later occupied by the comedian Bob Monkhouse. The map shows the settlement is on the ridge of the hill and the ancient road separates the parishes of Eggington and Stanbridge.*

for her support. She is then credited with using the wealth from her royal estates to rebuild and refurbish the great church at Wing – around 300 years after it was first built.

Aelfgyfu apparently died some time after A.D. 975, exactly when is not recorded although her will was made about then. The Linslade charter was attached to it. In the will she gave large grants of money and some land to the New Minster at Winchester, and her estates at Linslade, Wing and elsewhere to King Edgar. One interesting point in the will is the freeing of penal slaves on estates she gave to the church. Penal slavery was a way of punishing criminals who required royal consent to be made free.

The bounds of Linslade are described in the will in clockwise fashion starting at the village in the north and following the course of the river upstream to Tiddenfoot ford. The boundary then leaves the river and follows

24 *Edith, portrayed at her marriage to Edward the Confessor in January 1045. This last Queen of Saxon England owned Linslade. Her husband's death in 1066 resulted in William the Conqueror's invasion that year. Edith lived quietly on her estates and died at Winchester in 1075. She was buried 'with great honour' in Westminster Abbey next to King Edward.*

the now disappeared ancient Thiodweg up the hill towards Wing. It is a recipe for getting thoroughly lost but a translation of the will reads:

> From Linslade (the river crossing by the lynch) along the river to the ford of the Yttingas. From the ford along the street to Tunbeald's tree. From that tree along the street onto the midmost hill. From that hill along the street to seven mounds. From seven mounds to the one mound. From the one mound to the barley croft, to the upper end of it. From the upper end into the middle of the boundary valley, to the riddy. From the riddy by the headlands of the acres to the old dyke. Along the dyke back again within the stream.

From the description it seems that even at this time Linslade was a farmed landscape although the origin of the hills or mounds and whether they are man-made is unexplained.

By this time the so-called Dark Ages are drawing to a close. The next important date for Leighton Buzzard and indeed all of Britain is 1066. The last of the old royal line of Wessex kings, Edward the Confessor, died in January that year. His successor, Harold, to survive, had first had to fight and defeat the invading

Danes at the battle of Stamford Bridge outside York and then march south again to take on William of Normandy in Sussex. Among his followers would have been men from Leighton and Linslade, both by then part of a series of royal estates that stretched across the area from Luton. The close-run second battle ended in Harold's death. Many of his leading subjects died too, including some who owned land close to Leighton.

Following his victory at Hastings, William marched north-west and crossed the Thames at Wallingford then swung north to Berkhamsted, meeting the remaining English nobles there, where they submitted and acknowledged him as king. This must have been a traumatic time for England and much land changed hands as William rewarded his followers and imposed his will on all who resisted. He laid waste much of the north but it seems that the Leighton area, in new royal hands, fared better. Domesday Book records these changes, as the new order asserts its control over England.

3
The Land of the King

Domesday Book of 1086, William the Conqueror's assessment of what his new kingdom was worth for the purpose of levying tax, is also the best way for historians to find out the status, population and general activities of the people who lived in the countryside. Leighton Buzzard recorded as Lestone in this remarkable document, with its market, was the focus of a wealthy royal estate. Its importance is clear because after the county town of Bedford it comes first in the entry for Bedfordshire under the heading 'The Land of the King'.

Another bonus of Domesday Book is that it was completed 20 years after the conquest and compares the worth of the country in 1086 with the value and ownership of estates before William invaded, in the time of the last Saxon King, Edward the Confessor. Of course, the language and units of measurement used take some understanding. Leighton was assessed as 47 hides – a hide is generally held to be the land needed to provide a living for an extended family for a year. The royal manor was also said to have land for 52 ploughs. This

is again a measurement, this time of arable land. Land for one plough is supposed to be an area that one team of eight oxen with a plough attached would manage to turn over in a day. There was also meadowland sufficient for 42 ploughteams, in other words, to keep 42 lots of eight oxen in fodder for the year, plus woodland for 100 swine. This last figure is small for a manor of Leighton's size, Luton for example, had enough woods for 1,000 swine.

Historians therefore conclude that the Leighton of Domesday was largely arable land with valuable meadowland alongside the Ouzel and Clipstone Brook. There was also a little woodland up at Heath and Reach where the ancient and aptly named King's Wood still stands. Experts also surmise that this open farmed landscape had been the picture since before the Conquest, because unusually the value of Leighton for tax purposes remained unchanged from Edward's day. In many parts of the country, especially in the north where there had been stout resistance to the Norman Conquest, the army had laid waste to many

25 *Domesday Book entry for Leighton, the first time the name Leighton appears in the historic record. It paints a picture of a busy, thriving market town owned by the King of England.*

areas. Many manors had not recovered and were worth less than half their previous value. Some had almost no taxable assets in 1086.

Leighton had changed in one respect, however. The king had not owned all the estate in Edward's time. The king's chamberlain, called Wenesi, had owned 10 hides, and Starcher, a thane, the Saxon equivalent of a knight, another seven hides. Their fate is not discussed in Domesday Book but both were probably killed at the Battle of Hastings. William's sheriff had evidently annexed their land to Edward's former estate.

The Leighton manor included a large area between the A5 and the River Ouzel and although the places are not named they will have included the hamlets of Billington, Eggington, Stanbridge, Heath and Reach, then two settlements.

Domesday Book also recorded 82 villagers, 30 smallholders and two slaves living on the manor. Each had different rights and privileges under the feudal system, although the slaves, or serfs, had virtually none and no land. The rest would have their own land holdings as tenants, although some were very small. All those registered were men and were the heads of families. Their dependents were not mentioned but from the information provided it is possible to calculate the population in 1086, probably a maximum for the whole Leighton area of 630 people, almost all of whom would have been working on the land.

There was also a mill, classed as two mills because it had two sets of millstones. Later records say one set of stones was for grinding corn and one for malting barley used for making ale.

Most important for the King was how much the manor was worth in cash and goods. We learn that the town had a market because the tolls paid by people buying and selling animals and goods were £7 for the year, the largest sum in Bedfordshire for a market. The two mills were worth 30s. in taxes. In all, the estate was said to yield £22 in weighed money in tax and portions of wheat and honey in lieu of cash. For the Queen's use there were two ounces of gold, and one ounce of gold

for the sheriff. One curiosity was the 70s. for the 'lawing of the dogs'. This was a levy for the removal of claws from the feet of dogs so they could not be used for hunting the king's deer.

One other landholding in Leighton was four hides owned by the Church, in this case the Bishop of Lincoln, within whose diocese Leighton came. This was another hangover from Saxon times when Bishop Wulfwig held this land during the time of King Edward. The Saxon bishop had been replaced by a Norman one by 1086 but the land still remained in the hands of the Church. These four hides are believed to be the land surrounding All Saints, the current parish church, and almost certainly contained a church then, although no building is recorded in Domesday Book since no tax is payable on churches. Linslade, on the other side of the Ouzel in Buckinghamshire, had also been a royal estate. It is recorded for tax purposes as 15 hides. It was no longer in royal ownership in 1086 but had been given to one of William's knights, Hugh de Beauchamp, presumably as reward for services rendered

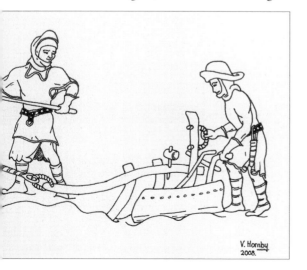

26 Oxen, not horses, provided the pulling power for ploughs in this period and were arranged in teams of eight. The water meadows bordering the Ouzel were a valued resource, providing fodder for these essential animals.

.XXV. **Terra Hvgonis De Belcamp.** *In Corteshala Hvnd.*

Hvco de belcamp ten̄ *Lincelada*.p̄ xv. hiđ
se defđ. Tra. c̄. xvi. car̄. In dn̄io. v. hidæ. ⁊ ibi fuꝓ
.ii. car̄. ⁊ adhuc. iii. poꝰ fieri. Ibi. xxii. uilti cū. vi. borđ
hn̄t. xi. car̄. Ibi. v. ferui. ⁊ i. molin de. xx. fot. p̄tū
.ii. car̄. Int̄ tot ual. x. liƀ. Q̄do recep̄: c̄. fot. T.R.E.
x. liƀ. Hoc m̄ tenuit Aluuin h̄ō Eddiđ regine. ⁊ uenđe pot,
In Soleberie ten̄ Hugo. ii. part uni uirḡ. Tra. c̄. iiii.
boƀ. Val ⁊ ualuit. iii. fot. T.R.E. iiii. fot. Hanc tram
tenuit Dor h̄ō đei. potuit uenđe cui uoluit.

27 Linslade's Domesday entry. It is a smaller estate than Leighton but had belonged to the former Queen of England, Edith, the widow of the Saxon king, Edward the Confessor. She was treated with respect by William and kept her estates until her death in 1075.

in defeating the English. The previous Saxon owner was recorded as 'Alwin, Queen Edith's man'. Here in 1086 there were 22 villagers, six smallholders, five slaves and a mill. Although the site of this is not known the mill could be in the water meadows near where the *Globe Inn* and Corbetts Hill Farm now stand. The total value of the estate was £10. No woodland is recorded.

There is an adjoining estate called 'Gladley' where there was enough land for one plough, woodland for 100 swine and a mill valued at

16s. This mill is believed to be Grange Mill, on the Old Linslade Road. The value of this holding had reduced since the time of King Edward, which could be neglect rather than any act of war. It seems the estate may have been a single farm. The farm still exists nearly 1,000 years later and is now called Nares Gladley Farm. The wood which supported 100 swine is thought to be the same recorded as being cut down and all the wood used up when the death of the tenant Geoffrey de Lucy was recorded in 1346.

A year after the Domesday recording began William died. His successors continued the battle for control of the English crown and the fate and fortunes of Leighton changed again during the almost forgotten civil wars between William the Conqueror's grandchildren, Matilda and Stephen, when the royal lands were fought over and neglected.

Matilda's son Henry II finally succeeded to the throne in 1154 and had to sort out the kingdom's estates and depleted coffers. One of his immediate problems was the generous annual cash gift of £60 his grandfather Henry I had granted to the new Abbey of Fontevrault in Anjou in France's Loire Valley. Henry I had made the cash grant to the Abbey because, at the death of his only son, his young daughter-in-law Matilda had become a nun there, and subsequently

the Abbess. This was still a time when the Norman kings felt that England was alien soil, and during their rule were more likely to send their relatives to enter religious houses and shower gifts on establishments on the opposite side of the Channel. In 1164, however, Henry II obviously had other needs for his depleted amount of ready cash than sending it to Fontevrault, so in lieu of cash gave the Abbey his royal estate of Leighton.

The income from the manor, with a few additions of land from elsewhere, was estimated to equal the value of the cash gift and so Henry could not be accused of short changing the Abbey. The reality, however, was different. Because of the civil wars the Leighton estate had apparently been badly run down and was in need of careful management to restore its productivity.

The Anjou abbey was a mixed order of nuns and monks who eventually established six priories in England. They responded to Henry's gift by sending a group of monks to found a priory in Leighton. This was a small church with living quarters attached for the monks. The site was not in Leighton but on raised ground south of the town beyond Tiddenfoot at La Grava, better known as Grovebury, where the Saxons had once built a great hall. It is not known whether there were pre-existing buildings on the site when they arrived, but as well as building their modest priory the monks added farm buildings to create a new manorial centre, making the most out of what must have been potentially a productive agricultural estate. To get the monks started, the abbey in France spent more than £5 on animals to restock the estate.

28 *Grange Mill, mentioned in the Domesday entry for Gladley, a small estate on the opposite side of the Ouzel from Old Linslade. This modern picture is of the current mill building, now a private house.*

29 *The fishponds at La Grava, known locally as Grovebury. These ensured a supply of fresh fish to the monastic kitchens, essential because of religious edicts on meat eating. These modern pictures were taken when the river was in flood but show the extent of the ponds, which were an early example of sophisticated fish farming.*

One of the reasons for choosing this site might have been the extensive potential for fish farming. A series of fishponds alongside the Ouzel can still be seen and are the only remaining features of this site that have not been lost to sand quarrying. The existing town to the north, clustered round the church, was presumably considered too worldly for the monks, who needed a quieter location.

Among the innovations at La Grava was a windmill, which must have been one of the earliest in England. All mills mentioned in Domesday Book were water mills. Windmills were invented in the Middle East, probably Persia, and first spotted by European crusader knights. The first record of a European windmill was in Normandy in 1180. It is not known exactly when the Grovebury mill was built but in 1212 the Prior was having a dispute with the locals over putting up the price of grinding corn in his windmill. The monks appear to have imported this new technology. The site of the windmill was on top of an Iron-Age burial mound, and its stump could still be seen until the whole Grovebury area was destroyed by sand workings in the 1990s. Fortunately an extensive archaeological dig over 20 years uncovered many of the secrets of the site. More than 100 buildings were discovered, their uses understood and their history traced as they were developed and then allowed to decay or actively destroyed over succeeding centuries.

30 *St Mary's, Linslade, possibly built on the site of a Saxon church, now isolated but once the centre of a thriving market town where pilgrims flocked to visit the nearby Holy Well.*

While the monks were working to restore the wealth of their new estate, the village opposite Leighton on the other side of the Ouzel was thriving.

The descendants of William's knight, Hugh de Beauchamp, continued to own the Linslade estate and village. His grandson, Payn de Beauchamp, who owned other large estates in Bedfordshire, followed the Norman tradition of religious endowments and founded Chicksands Priory in 1144; a large part of this building still stands although one of the oldest remaining buildings was much altered when used as the officers' quarters of an American air base.

Payn's son Simon is credited with building St Mary's, the sandstone church in Old Linslade which would then have been, with the manor house, at the centre of the village. This is dated around 1165, when Simon came of age. Unlike most churches it still has a simple nave and chancel, without side aisles added. Apart from the porch and the

BEAUCHAMP of Bedford. *Quarterly or and gules a bend sable.*

31 *The arms of Hugh de Beauchamp, one of William's knights, who was given the manor at Linslade after Queen Edith's death. The de Beauchamps became Barons of Bedford, and held extensive estates throughout the county.*

32-4 *The interior of St Mary's is virtually unchanged since it was first built in the 12th century. The Chancel Arch still has traces of paint from the once vibrant decorations of the church and the early font, with its encircling mythical beasts, is a splendid and rare survival of early Norman carving.*

15th-century tower, St Mary's has hardly been enlarged since it was built. It is the oldest building in Leighton or Linslade. The chancel arch dates from the early period as does the font, which is a particularly splendid example of the Aylesbury style thought to date to around 1210.

The age of the church can be fixed because Simon confirms the grant of the revenues of Linslade church to the new priory at Chicksands in a document dated between 1165-79. The priory received the great tithes from the parish and was responsible for appointing the vicar. In the 13th century the village of Linslade was in its heyday with an increasing population. In 1251 a market and eight-day fair was granted to William de Beauchamp, the current lord of the manor, who was obviously planning to expand his village into a market town. The fair was held on the eve and feast day of the Nativity of St Mary, 8 September, and the six days following. The market day was Thursday.

The prosperity of Linslade was probably partly due to the popularity of the Holy Well, a short walk from the church. This is marked on old Ordnance Survey maps. Pilgrims flocked to the well, which was thought to have healing properties, and the visitors brought in trade and money. The vicar encouraged the pilgrimages, but things got so out of hand that in 1299 the Bishop of Lincoln, Oliver Sutton, issued an order banning the practice and calling the vicar to appear before the Archdeaconry Court. However, pilgrimages may not have stopped altogether; as late as 1502 the Queen of England knew of 'our lady of Linchelade' and sent offerings, and there was still a path through Wing towards Linslade known as St Mary's Way, a street name preserved in the modern town of Linslade.

While Linslade was thriving Leighton seems to have declined. This may in part be due to Henry I's decision to found a new town only 10 miles away at Dunstable at the junction of the old Roman Road Watling Street and the even more ancient east-west route Icknield Way. There had been a town here still in Roman times but it had been abandoned under the Saxons who preferred to live on the hilltops. Dunstable is not mentioned in Domesday Book although nearby Houghton

Regis is recorded as the centre of a royal estate. Henry set up a new Dunstable with a market at this ancient crossroads and it grew into a thriving town.

As with Domesday Book, a picture of the relative prosperity of various places emerges from the tax return of 1297. It records 122 taxpayers in Dunstable, 47 of whom are merchants. The same return shows 118 taxpayers in the much older parish and town of Leighton, of whom only 16 are not classed as agricultural. Just as interesting is that almost all these Leighton merchants are listed in the comparatively small church estate of four hides which was recorded in Domesday Book. Leighton's enormous and almost cathedral-like All Saints Church had been built just before this. It is first recorded in 1277 and is described as being finished in 1288.

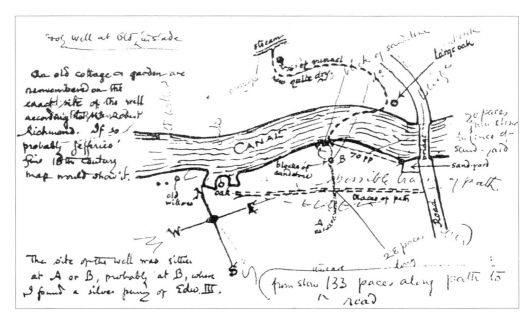

35 *The site of the Holy Well, illustrated in a map drawn in 1915 by Frederick Gurney, a local historian from Eggington. He shows the well in two places but says it is probably on the edge of the reed bed next to the canal where he saw a sandstone block and found a silver penny of Edward III.*

36-7   *The spire of All Saints, Leighton can be seen for miles around. Its grandeur is probably due to the ownership by the Bishop of Lincoln of the estate surrounding the church. The income from the estate paid for a prebend, who was an official of Lincoln Cathedral. But this ownership also brought patronage, and a wealthy prebend, Nicholas de Heigham, who died in 1288, left 'sufficient of his goods' to complete the church.*

38   *The font at All Saints, which probably pre-dates the present church and is Early English design. One of the treasures of All Saints in this early period was part of the tunic of St Hugh, who was a venerated Bishop of Lincoln from 1186 until his death in 1200.*

So it is clear that by 1297 All Saints has become the focus of the town and it seems likely that Church Square, laid out on church-owned land, was surrounded by shops and probably provided space for the market.

The Prebendal Manor, as the church estate had become, with its own manor house as a residence for the prebend, the official representative of the Lincoln diocese, had 25 taxpayers living within its borders, 13 of whom were paying tax on unspecified merchandise, utensils and copper vessels. Remarkably, among them are two women: Margery Faber's name is latin for smith, so perhaps she is running a smithy; and Fina la Teynturesse appears to be trading as a dyer. The rest of the parish, which is owned by the French abbey and run by the local priory, seems to have been concentrating on agriculture and not trade.

One of the key unanswered questions about Leighton is the date of the first bridge across the Ouzel towards Linslade. In Saxon times it was clear that the major crossing of the river was the ford at Tiddenfoot where Thiodweg crossed, hence the 906 treaty which places this site as the boundary between the Saxons and Danelaw. But in 1311 there is mention in documents of the need to repair the bridges across the Ouzel, which indicates a bridge that must have been there long enough to need repair. The presence of a bridge at this early date would account for the decline of the ancient Thiodweg and the diversion of east-west travellers through Leighton. Presumably it was safer and easier to use the new bridge at Leighton rather than the old ford. This crossing would also have increased the possibilities of trade for Leighton merchants based next to the church and bridge.

The main manor of Leighton had now been in the hands of Fontevrault for more than a century. During this time it had undergone a series of building phases with the original timber being replaced by grander buildings of stone. These were of

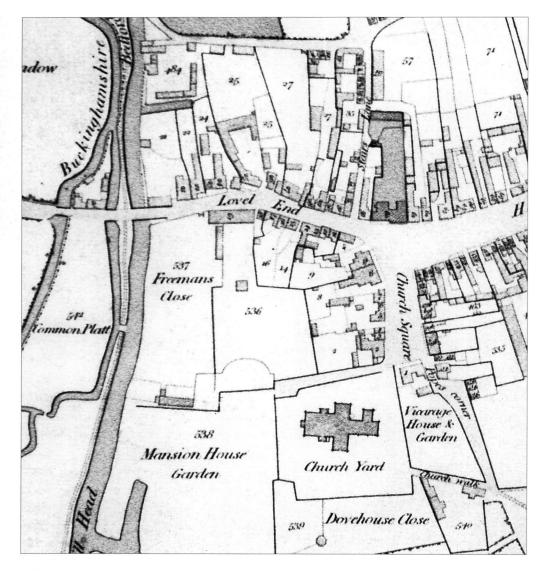

39 *A section of the 1819 map of the town by Benjamin Bevan, the son of the engineer to the Grand Junction Canal, showing the area around Church Square, believed to be the extent of the original Saxon town of Leighton.*

sufficient quality to accommodate visitors of high rank. Apart from the occasional record of manorial disputes with tenants, the life of the manor seems to have been untroubled, that is until national events again intervened.

Periodic hostilities with France over the English monarch's claim to the French throne had not at first troubled the 'alien' priory at Leighton, but during the war of 1293-1303 all of Fontevrault's properties in England were taken into the king's hands. This was a pattern that was to be repeated for the next 150 years when the priory named in documents as La Grava, and the Manor of Leighton, were frequently retained by the king during repeated wars. The manor was still technically owned by Fontevrault and the king handed the estate back again as soon as peace was restored.

These constant confiscations seemed to coincide with a reduced religious role for Grovebury and an increasingly royal interest in the establishment. A number of important documents were signed and dated by successive kings at Grovebury indicating that it was at least a regular stopover for royal progresses.

The first and perhaps most colourful of the tenants of Grovebury was Mary of Woodstock, the daughter of Edward I and sister of Edward II. She had become a nun as a child, a frequent practice in the medieval period. She held the Leighton manor as tenant of Fontevrault from 1305 to her death in 1332. Mary was not a shy, retiring and pious nun but frequently travelled the country on horseback or by chariot with a large entourage and spent vast sums of money given to her by her indulgent father, Edward I, and subsequently her brother when in turn he became King Edward II. She was sent large quantities of wood, fish and wine by her father and brother and appears to have been a compulsive gambler. Despite her considerable income she seems to have frequently run out of cash at the gaming tables and is reported to have borrowed money from her servants to continue.

For some of the time she lived at Grovebury and was probably in residence

40-1   *Edward II's effigy on his tomb in Gloucester Cathedral. He reigned from 1307 to 1327 and was a frequent visitor to Leighton. The coin showing his head (below) was found in 2005 at Heath and Reach.*

when Edward II visited repeatedly between 1308 and 1310. His visits are confirmed by the number of documents signed there. He is known to have stayed for three weeks at a time and, it is thought, was visiting the sister on whom he lavished gifts.

42 *A rare survival from the possessions of Mary of Woodstock, a travelling candlestick found during excavations at Grovebury.*

and industrial buildings such as a latrine block, dairy, smokehouse for preserving fish, kitchens and workshops. There were also ovens, kilns and drains showing a sophisticated and busy enterprise. Among the many finds by archaeologists on the site was a rare and expensive travelling candlestick carrying royal arms, believed to be those of Mary of Woodstock.

The frequent use of Grovebury by successive monarchs, including Edward III, who stayed in 1337, was due to the fact that Leighton was a convenient stop-off point on the way north. King's Langley in Hertfordshire, which was also a popular royal residence, is a day's ride to the south. The close association with both royalty and Fontevrault continued. Maud de Burgh, Countess of Ulster, daughter of the powerful Duke of Lancaster, was the lady of the manor from 1338. In 1357 Edward III's daughter, Isabel, was granted the safekeeping of all Fontevrault's lands in England, including Leighton, because of the renewal of the war with France.

Alice Chaucer, the great English poet's granddaughter, who became Alice de la Pole, Duchess of Suffolk, inherited the manor in 1415 on the death of her first husband at the Battle of Agincourt. The Fontevrault, or French, connection finally came to an end after 250 years when Henry V appropriated all alien priories in 1414. The site at La Grava gradually declined and eventually became a sheep farm.

In October 1309 when the King was at Grovebury an unfortunate incident occurred. The Calendar of Patent Rolls records 'that Philip de Wavendon, whilst on the King's service guarding one of his horses, lost an ear by its bite'.

It is clear that by this time Grovebury was a large establishment with monastic buildings and a chapel, timber and stone halls, chamber blocks, a refectory, and domestic

4

The Black Death and the Buzzard

While the manor of Leighton was swapping ownership between a French abbey and the kings of England, the people of Leighton Buzzard and the villages in the parish continued farming. The Black Death was soon to sweep across England causing a population crash, but until that calamity the feudal system of peasants owing allegiance and labour to their lords continued unchanged.

The Domesday return had not mentioned any other settlement apart from Leighton because the whole estate, including Grovebury, was all part of the same parish, but it seems certain that separate communities had existed since Saxon times. The earliest hamlet names mentioned are Stanbridge in 1165, Eggington and Clipstone in 1195, Billington in 1196, Reach in 1216 and Heath in 1220. These last two settlements were separate, although less than half a mile apart. Linslade was a single parish, also, but much smaller. It had one separate hamlet south of the main village, first mentioned as Southcott in 1240.

The parish churches of St Mary's in Linslade and All Saints, Leighton Buzzard,

were the only places local people could be baptised, married or buried. The villages and other settlements subsequently had their own churches or chapels but these were for day-to-day services and Sunday worship only. The right to conduct the services for the three most important rituals of the church were reserved to the parish churches, and with them went the lucrative fees charged by the clergy.

In other respects these settlements operated as separate communities and would have had an agricultural system based on strip farming. Tenants were allocated some strips on good land and some on poor. These strips were ploughed so the soil was heaped in the middle with a valley marking the border in between. In some unploughed pastures this field pattern can still be seen today in what is called ridge and furrow. Animals were both precious possessions and hard to feed in the winter, so grazing rights on common land and water meadows were jealously guarded. There were strict rules about haymaking for winter fodder and when animals could be turned onto the open fields to forage after

43 *The remnants of Stanbridge's medieval ridge and furrow system of strip farming show up clearly in this 1974 aerial picture taken at sunset. The ridges are only preserved because the giant common fields were fenced, grassed over and used for grazing sheep. At the time of this photograph they had not been ploughed since enclosure.*

the harvest. On the 'wastes', or heathland, around Leighton and Linslade, the right to gather firewood or stone for building was also an important factor in the local economy.

Crops appeared to be a wider mixture than today, with wheat being the most valuable because it was used for the best bread. In 1341 the crops were recorded in Leighton as being 45 per cent wheat, 29 per cent oats, 17 per cent dredge (a mixture of barley and oats) and 8 per cent peas and beans.

Linslade on the other hand appears to have grown a lot of rye, about seventy per cent of the total crop at some times. These mixtures puzzle historians. Obviously some were used for winter fodder for the oxen used for ploughing and for the heavy farm horses, some were used to keep the sheep and pigs alive over the winter, and enough was kept for seed the following year. Rye was used for

poorer quality bread and some believe that for the dry sandy soils of Linslade this was the best available crop, although some areas like Southcott had clay.

The fields at Grove, where the priory farmed, were better quality although the land north of Leighton was also poor. The townsfolk would also have farmed strips with two or three large fields worked on a communal system. It seems, however, from the layout of the town and the tax returns, that a trading community had already developed close to the parish church and the river crossing. The residents were supplementing their farming income by trade.

As we have seen earlier, the bridge across the Ouzel at Leighton was in need of repair by 1311, so one was almost certainly in existence in 1297 when the first detailed list of people who lived and traded in the town appears in a tax return. This is not a full list of residents but only includes the wealthiest members of the community. Those with less than 9s. worth of disposable property were exempt from tax.

There were 49 taxpayers in Leighton town, another 18 at Heath, 13 at Billington, 11 at Clipstone and a surprising 27 at Eggington, possibly better off than most because of the continued use of the ancient Thiodweg trading route that ran through the village.

As we saw in the last chapter, the Leighton merchants were mostly crowded round the church in the Prebendal Manor. Their shops were probably along what is now Bridge Street and Church Square on the route that everyone would have to travel to reach Buckinghamshire and the west on the all-important bridge across the Ouzel.

The listed names give us an insight into the trades of the taxpayers but also the first glimpse of the use of surnames, and how they developed. So Alan Spicer, who had 10s. worth of merchandise on his tax list, was almost certainly a dealer in spices. John Glovere had 2s. worth of utensils, presumably for making gloves, and Margery Faber had 2s. 6d. of utensils, probably in the forge. In this period widows normally carried on the business of their late husbands.

There were three men called Mercator, Stephen, Elias and Richard, possibly not related but given that surname because they were in trade. In a town where all the buildings apart from the church are likely to be of wood, wattle and daub, William Carpentarious would be a vital member of the community.

There is another Glovere, and an Agnes Taylur, giving more clues to the trades competing for custom. The name of John

Brekepot, who is taxed on a foal, two heifers and a quarter of rye, shows that characteristics other than trade helped to make up the new surnames.

Two further tax returns of 1309 and 1332 show the number of trades developing and with them other descriptive surnames. There is Richard Irenmongere and Hugh and Richard le Fullere, these last two obviously men working in the cloth trade.

One man listed under Heath is Robert Molendinario, Latin for miller. The only mill in Heath was what is now called Grange Mill, so his profession also helps to locate where he may have lived.

Other surnames are derived from places. Local ones include Simon de Brickhill, Will de Flutewyk, John de Potsgrave and, from slightly further away, John de Huntingdone. It is also clear that the attraction of Leighton as a town, market and trading centre was growing because two probable French residents and traders, John le Freynsche and Henry le Freynsce, were paying taxes. The clerk's different renderings of 'Frenchy' were typical of the relaxed attitude to spelling of the time. John le Rede and Matilda Reyner probably had red hair, and Cristina de Pratis would translate as Christine Meadows.

The frequently changing spelling of names is often attributed to clerks from distant places like London and Lincoln trying to write down phonetically local pronunciation. Whatever the reason, there is an extraordinary range of 60 spellings of Leighton down the centuries, and 40 of Buzzard.

The Lestone of Domesday was probably derived from the Saxon Leacton, a kitchen

44 *Ancient graffiti on the south-west pier of the tower of All Saints Church, dating from soon after 1400, to judge by the costumes of the man and woman depicted. Local legend has it that this is Simon and Nell disagreeing over the way to cook the first simnel cake. This is a traditional cake originally eaten in mid-Lent.*

garden, or Leah, field or meadow. Lestone was never spelt the same way again after Domesday and had evolved by 1393 into Leyetone. Although there were interesting variations, which sometimes included 'z's and 'x's, the general sound of Leighton remained through the centuries thereafter.

The Buzzard is altogether a different problem. In many parts of the country place names derive from the landed families who owned the manor. In this case it seems it is the church's ownership of the centre of Leighton that is the reason for the Buzzard. In the 13th century there were two Leightons in the diocese of Lincoln, one in Huntingdonshire and our own.

The diocese had to distinguish between the two and it is in a deed dated 1242 that the name Busard appears for the first time. A Theobald de Bosat, also spelt de Busar, was Canon of Lincoln Cathedral, although he also lived for some time in Leighton. Another, later, document describes this churchman as 'Parson' of the church of Leighton at the time of King Richard I. It seems that during de Busar's time, Lincoln Cathedral scribes took to calling the town Leighton Busar to distinguish it from Leighton Bromswold in Huntingtonshire. The first Buzzard spelling appeared in 1526 and disappeared again but eventually triumphed over the other 39 contenders.

One local person who does not appear in the tax returns but whose skill as a craftsman is his claim to fame is Thomas of Leighton. His foliate wrought-iron hinges appear on the west door of Leighton Buzzard's church and also at Turvey. His greatest and best-known work was in 1293-4 when he made the ornate ironwork for Queen Eleanor's tomb in Westminster Abbey. The accounts record a payment of £13 to

Master Thomas de Leghton, smith, for ironwork about the tomb of the Queen at Westminster, and for the carriage of the same

45 (Left) The door of All Saints Church, Leighton Buzzard showing the intricate scroll work in iron by Thomas of Leighton which dates from about 1290. He was nationally famous for his skill and employed by the widowed King Edward I to build the ornate screen around Queen Eleanor's tomb in Westminster Abbey in 1294.

46 (Above) Detail from All Saints' door highlighting the ironwork.

from Legton to London and the expenses of the said Thomas and his men dwelling in London to place the said ironwork about the tomb aforesaid.

Although Thomas is not mentioned in tax returns, a number of ironmongers and what appears to be an iron miner are mentioned over the following centuries. This, combined with archaeological evidence uncovered from Chamberlain's Barn Saxon cemetery excavations, and other references, seem to show that ironstone mined and smelted locally provided raw material for skilled craftsmen and merchants.

This apparent success of Leighton as a trading centre and crossing point of the river appears to have stimulated one of the town's lords of the manor to develop the town. This could have been an entrepreneurial Abbess of Fontevrault, one of the royal lessees when the manor was in the hands of the Crown, or the Bishop of Lincoln, but whoever it was took the decision to capitalise on the growing prosperity to lay out the now familiar wide High Street and large market place. The market was later encroached on by shops and a market hall but originally would have been a very large space. Shops were laid out as they are now with North Street and Lake Street forming a Y-shape. The

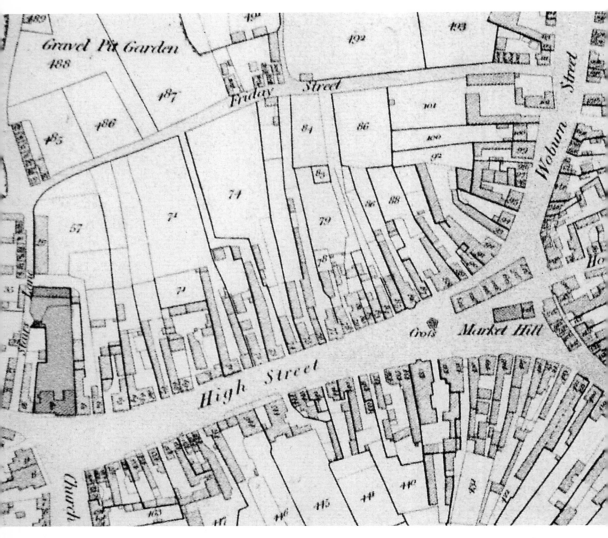

47 *An enlargement of part of the map produced by Benjamin Bevan. It is dated 1819 and clearly shows the burgage plots on the north side of the High Street. Behind the buildings these long yards would have been used for workshops and stabling.*

original Church Square and slightly winding Bridge Street appear to pre-date this 14th-century new town layout.

Development of new towns was not uncommon in this period when the population of England appears generally to have been rising. It had probably reached around four million when, in 1349, disaster struck in the form of the bubonic plague or Black Death. Records are sparse for the period but the loss of life was so great that it led to fundamental changes in the relationship between peasants and their masters. Between one third and a half of the population were wiped out.

The disease had arrived in the country the year before at Melcombe Regis, now a suburb

48 *The front of three properties on the north side of High Street, Leighton, a photograph taken in the 1890s. Each building plot has a standard width of 22 feet, the original width of the burgage plots when the medieval town was laid out. Many of the High Street properties have the same valuable frontage onto the market to this day.*

of Weymouth, carried across Europe by the fleas that live on black rats. It spread rapidly across England with the rats, which thrived in the wattle and daub houses and barns. The peasants died in huge numbers although nobody knew why for another 500 years when the link between the rat fleas and the disease was shown.

It was still 200 years before births, marriages and deaths were routinely recorded so what happened in Leighton and Linslade is not known precisely. However, in 1349 the diocese of Lincoln, of which Leighton and Linslade were part, replaced 77 clergy who died in that year, compared with an average of fourteen. Leighton had three vicars in 1349, and Linslade two, so it seems that both places were visited by the plague.

49 *A gateway at the side of Reid's shop, 19 High Street, still performing its original function of providing access to the yards and workshops behind the shop.*

50 *Plague graffiti scratched into the stonework on the door jamb of the original church door on the south side of St Mary's Church, Linslade. The lettering is medieval and is thought to be from the time of the Black Death. It was first recorded by Frederick Gurney in 1928. It appears to be a despairing appeal: 'a iesu helpe'. Note the medieval use of 'i' for the 'j' of Jesus.*

In Winslow, 10 miles from Leighton, some manorial records have been analysed. They show that in the village an average of five deaths of property holders were recorded in the years running up to 1349. In that year 161 property holder deaths are recorded, so many more members of their families and their households would also have died. In the following 30 years there were successive waves of plague across England. The death tolls were not so high during these outbreaks so perhaps some level of immunity had been reached, but by then the population had already dropped dramatically.

Leighton and each of the villages must have succumbed to at least some of these waves of pestilence. The result was that many families, often crowded together in tiny cottages, must have died out completely. A lot of manor court rolls of the period record property being passed to nephews and cousins because the immediate family no longer existed. This sudden loss of the working population meant peasants could expand their land holdings, and for the lords

of the manor the previously plentiful labour was in short supply.

The Black Death is credited with improving the lot of the survivors by allowing some peasants to work for wages instead of being under an obligation to their feudal lord to provide labour as part of their tenancy. There was also competition for peasants, with some manors so short of labour they were prepared to offer 'runaway' peasants from other areas land to farm.

During this period Linslade, which had previously prospered, now declined. This was probably mainly due to the banning of the pilgrimage to the Holy Well. Certainly the market had disappeared, because in the tax returns of 1327 there were 22 taxpayers but no merchants listed as living in the village. Compared with a more prosperous Leighton, Linslade was not a town of traders.

Obviously the area continued to be farmed and had illustrious tenants in the de Lucy family who lived some of the time at nearby Chelmscote. The last male of the line was Sir William de Lucy who was killed in a dastardly fashion at the Battle of Northampton on 10 July 1460. He was fighting on the Lancastrian side during the Wars of the Roses and the chronicler of the battle reports that after it was already over Sir John Stafford, who coveted 'his wife and hated him', took advantage of the situation and 'anon caused his death'. The widow, Lady Margaret de Lucy, did not take kindly to this act of unnecessary killing and married someone else, a Thomas Wake, a direct descendant of Hereward the Wake, the last Englishman to resist William the Conqueror.

Sir William de Lucy died childless but his niece, Elizabeth Hopton, inherited part of the Linslade estate. She married three times, each husband being rich and at times successful. The first died naturally but the last two fell from grace. On her second marriage Elizabeth became Countess of Worcester, but her husband was beheaded in 1470. Her final husband was Sir William Stanley, who was also executed in 1496. Her misfortune in losing husbands seems to have been Linslade's gain. She appears to have lived in the manor next to the church and is believed to have been religious, spending some of her fortune on building the church's 15th-century tower that still remains.

While Linslade's market died, the fortunes of Leighton's traders with their new market place were prospering. A market hall was built with a room above with a window looking west along the High Street. This room was used for town meetings, for the periodic manor court, and later as a school. Another fine building next to it was the hall of the Guild of Leighton Buzzard, otherwise known as the Fraternity Hall.

The Fraternity was a society of the great and good of the town. They had feast days and processions and paid for a chaplain at All Saints Church. The guild had a strong religious element. When members died the entire brotherhood turned out for the funeral. An early fraternity is mentioned in the 1440s, but there is a record of the founding of a second fraternity on 13 December 1473. At the time the influential Alice Chaucer was lady of the manor of the royal estate of Leighton. Alice's only child, John, Duke of Suffolk, was married to the sister of King Edward IV, who granted the licence for the new fraternity.

The founding charter says Alice Chaucer along with her son John and others can

establyshe and found a Fraternitye or Gyld for ever of ten wardens and ten brothers and systers in Layton Bussard and that the said wardens and brothers should have capacitie to take landes to the valewe of ten markes to the sustentacyon of a prest to syng daily in

51 *The Coat of Arms of the de Lucy family depicting three pikes or luce. A luce is a play on their name and is the Middle English term for a full grown pike. The family held the manor of Linslade under the de Beauchamps and other lords of the manor until the Wars of the Roses in the 15th century.*

LUCY. *Gules three luces or.*

52 *To the right of the Market Cross in this drawing of 1803 is the original timber-framed medieval Fraternity Hall. This is where the merchants of the town met to hold their Guild dinners. They were called the Fraternity of Corpus Christi and were wealthy enough to erect this building on one of the best sites in the town. They also provided funds for an extra priest at All Saints to minister to the people.*

53 *The Market Cross's date is not known but the style suggests the 15th century. Many believe it was built at the behest of Alice Chaucer when she was lady of the manor. During Cromwell's Commonwealth in the 1650s preachers used it to proclaim their Puritan message and in the fashion of the times marriage banns were proclaimed from the Cross on market days.*

the Churche of Layton for the good estate of the said Kyng Edward and Quene Elizabeth his wyff and the said Duchess and Duke of Suffolk: and for the sayd brothers and systers of the said Fraternytie whyle they were lyvying and for their soles when they were deceassed.

Evidence that Leighton was prosperous during this period is the building of the splendid Market Cross which with its elaborate stone carvings would have been

a costly gesture. After Alice's death in 1475 the manor, having lost all connections with France, passed to the newly established Dean and Canons of St George's Chapel at Windsor. Their first tenant was Leighton's last royal lady Cecily, the Duchess of York, mother to Edward IV and Richard III. When she died in Berkhamsted Castle in 1495, Leighton's royal connection ended. The next century would see Leighton in the hands of a new breed of men – the wealthy Tudor merchant.

5
A Spy and Civil War

Although the intrigues surrounding Henry VIII and his six wives are among the most written about episodes of English history, the traumatic effect these events had on the lives of ordinary people is hardly mentioned.

To obtain a divorce from his first wife, Catherine of Aragon, Henry made himself head of the Church in England. In doing so he set aside the supremacy of the Pope, who was referred to thereafter merely as the Bishop of Rome and saw his name erased from the prayer books. Not to acknowledge Henry as Head of the Church was treason and those with religious scruples about this paid with their lives. Among them was the Abbot of Woburn, Robert Hobbes, his sub-prior, Ralph Barnes, and another monk, Laurence Peck of Blunham. Their last minute repentance came too late and they were hanged from an oak tree at the Abbey gate in Woburn.

These executions were part of the suppression and dissolution of the monasteries, whose lands and goods were seized by the King. The lead was taken from the roofs and buildings were stripped, although some, like Dunstable Priory, were modified into parish churches, and others, including Woburn Abbey, were sold to favoured courtiers like John Russell to be turned into stately homes. His descendants still live at the Abbey.

Some churches were able to take advantage of Woburn's distress. For example, Wing churchwardens record the payment to carters for 'mete and drynke' to travel to Woburn to get 'A lowde of stuffe'. The stuff included the church organ, ornaments and a new window for Wing church.

Although Leighton Buzzard's French-controlled priory had closed by the mid-15th century, the link that Linslade had to the monastery at Chicksands had lasted until Henry's time. The oldest remaining memorial in Linslade church is to Agnes Aytoun, mother of John Aytoun, who was Prior of Chicksands and vicar of Linslade from 1480. In the Latin inscription on the brass the prior asks for blessings on the soul of his mother.

In around 1530 allegations of impropriety were made against the nuns at Chicksands, but it seems likely that even before this the lands at

Linslade had been confiscated by the Crown. In any event records show that by 1534 income from the church lands and tithes had been leased out to Philip Stryngar, his wife Alice and son John, who lived in Linslade parish.

Both Linslade and Leighton parish churches would have been full of statues and altars to various saints of the sort that can still be seen in Catholic churches on the continent. During the 1540s these symbols were removed from places of worship as the Puritans took over and the churches became plain. At the same time as the churches were undergoing this change, the Leighton Buzzard Fraternity with its chaplain and religious ceremonies was suppressed and its goods and hall confiscated.

The relatively small Linslade church of St Mary's, now almost completely plain, would once have had colourful wall paintings telling bible stories, the lives of the saints, and also depicting the torments of hell. The new Puritan edicts would have been to paint over these superstitious pictures with whitewash. Faint traces of the underlying coloured paint can still be seen on the chancel arch. The inventory of the church goods, dated 23 July 1552, lists a gilded silver chalice, gilded copper

cross and staff, candlesticks, embroidered silk cloths, bells, banners and streamers. The valuable metal objects would have been taken to the Tower of London and melted down.

This change in religious belief and style of worship also had a dramatic effect on the wills of the period. For centuries people had given property and money to the church for the good of their soul, hoping to shorten their time in purgatory. In 1520, for example, before the Reformation, John Esgoer, a wealthy cloth merchant of Leighton Buzzard who in his will asked to be buried in the churchyard at All Saints made a whole series of bequests as insurance for his soul. He left to Lincoln Cathedral, the 'mother church', 4d. and to the high altar at Leighton 8d. In addition he left valuable malt to be sold to provide money for wax candles to light the rood screen altar, the church's many other altars dedicated to individual saints, and also a contribution to the

54 *An original niche in All Saints Church built to hold a saint's statue. Underneath would have been an altar. All these were swept away in the Reformation. These niches were rediscovered in a church restoration of 1885. This one now holds a modern statue of the Virgin and Child, but in 1519 in John Esgoer's will he names altars to St Christopher, St Erasmus, St Appolome and Our Lady.*

wages of a priest to say a series of masses for his soul at the altar of the Virgin Mary. In addition to the malt, which was probably used to brew beer for church ale to be sold for funds, he left a pound of wax for 'lights', that is, candles, for all the saints:

> Item unto the maintenance of the rood light and St Christopher's light to each of them half a quarter of malt. Item to St Erasmus light half a quarter of malt. Item to the light of St Appolome two bushels of malt. Item a pound of wax to be divided among all the saints as to the small lights. Item to Our Lady's light in the North Aisle half a quarter of malt.

Leaving nothing to chance, he also left 20 cows, one each, to 20 local churches for a yearly mass to be said for his soul.

Esgoer was also a bit of a philanthropist and obviously cared about Leighton Buzzard because he left 14s. every year for 10 years from the rents of three houses in the North End (now North Street) to pay workmen to repair the road. He specifically ordered that out of this sum; 6s. was to be used for brewing ale at Whitsun, 4s. was for bread and 4s. for cheese to sustain the men for three days while the work was done. The curate of All Saints was to advertise the job each year and also tell potential road menders the victuals available.

The will also leaves Esgoer's shop to his wife Agnes and a portfolio of shops, houses and land to his family and godchildren. His son, Roger, gets his sheaf of arrows and bows and a woman, whose relationship to him is unknown but possibly the source of marital discord, gets free accommodation for life:

> I will that the tenement Sett in the lovett Ende [Bridge Street] in the which Isabell Rolf widoo in habiteth that after my deceas the said Isabell shall during her life dwell therein Rent free withoute any interuption or lett of my Wif.

In contrast, 29 years later in 1549, during the first year of the reign of Henry's only son, Edward VI, John Adams, a tenant of Linslade manor who wants his body buried in the churchyard, leaves nothing to the church fabric, or for candles, because these practices have been swept away. Instead he leaves 3s. 4d. to the 'poore mens boxe' in the church and then names 28 neighbours who live in Linslade and Southcott, all of whom are left 4d. each. Other bequests to family members are as much as £3 6s. 8d. each.

55 *Another drawing of the market place, showing the town hall and on the left the Leighton Fraternity building after it was converted to the Cross Keys pub. The Fraternity was dissolved in 1547. At the time it owned property in Lake Street and seven acres in Heath. Its property and jewels were seized by the Crown.*

56 *One of the few remaining thatched buildings in the town, Coopers Farm at Southcott in Linslade. After the village around St Mary's Church at Old Linslade declined and disappeared, probably during the 16th century, the hamlet of Southcott continued to thrive and had 18 farms. The land in this area is not so sandy and is more fertile. Hidden in the roof of this farmhouse is a medieval window.*

As mentioned previously, the manor of Leighton Buzzard had been given to the Dean and Canons of St George's Chapel, Windsor. Although the chapel was part of the royal castle complex, there were no more royal tenants or residents of the Leighton manor. The new owners charged with raising revenue for their chapel made the most of the potential income from the Leighton property by leasing it out to the new breed of Tudor merchants who had made their money in the City of London. These men wanted to invest their profits from trade in land and so leased and ran country estates. One of these new entrepreneurs of the Tudor age was Christopher Hoddesdon, who has an extraordinary history.

Hoddesdon was born in 1534, when Henry VIII was married to Anne Boleyn, and was the son of a yeoman from Little Stanmore in Middlesex. At 14 he was apprenticed to George Barne, who was an alderman of the City of London, a cloth merchant and member of the prestigious Haberdashers' Guild. Barne became Lord Mayor in 1553 and was one of a group of city merchants who set up a company to trade with Russia, at the time ruled by Ivan the Terrible. Two years later Christopher found himself sailing up the North Sea heading for Russia as Barne's agent in the Muscovy Company. It was a hazardous route round the north of Norway to the White Sea. He stayed in Russia for eight years and was head of the English delegation in Moscow for two of those, an extraordinary pioneering venture for a young man. On his return he married his master's granddaughter, Alice. By coincidence, Queen Elizabeth's future spymaster, Francis Walsingham, later married Alice's widowed mother and the fortunes of the two men became interlinked.

As Walsingham's career progressed under Elizabeth, so did that of Christopher Hoddesdon. He too became a cloth merchant, a member of the Haberdashers' Guild and an alderman of London, but also one of Walsingham's network of spies, using his trading ventures and travel in Europe as cover.

By 1566 Hoddesdon had come to the Queen's attention and was described in a letter from her to the Kings of Denmark and Sweden as 'a merchant of London and a man indeed of renowned trust and worth'. Such high status letters were carried as a form of early passport to ensure safe passage in foreign lands.

In 1577 it is clear that Hoddesdon has added the role of spy to his trading activities because he is sending information back to Lord Burghley, Elizabeth's principal minister. Hoddesdon, like Walsingham, was a strict Protestant and anti-Catholic. A letter describes the activities of an Englishman in Rome, who Hoddesdon claims was working as a spy for the Pope.

At the age of 48 in 1582, six years before the Spanish Armada attacked England, Hoddesdon had made sufficient money to buy the lease of Leighton Buzzard manor. At first, like previous merchant owners of the town, he continues to live in London and let out the Prebendal Manor House to a local butcher, but

documents show that seven years later he had moved to the town himself.

Hoddesdon's connection with the Walsingham family continued. His son was named Francis and his daughter, Ursula, after Walsingham's second wife.

This Tudor self-made man, and spy turned country gentleman, became Sheriff of Bedfordshire in 1591 and set about exploiting the estate. He apparently attempted to ride roughshod over what his tenants regarded as their ancient rights and privileges. He enclosed copses and common land to create a large rabbit warren – rabbits were then a rare and expensive delicacy and at the time were thought to need carefully constructed warrens to encourage them to breed. Court records

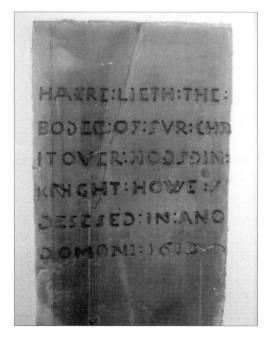

57 *The inscribed cover of Christopher Hoddesdon's coffin. It now hangs in the south transept of All Saints Church where it was found under the floor in 1840 along with the stone coffins of other members of the Leigh and Hoddesdon families.*

show that the tenants, women and men, turned up armed with 'guns, bows, bills, pikes, staves and pitchforks' and assembled 'riotously rowteously and unlawfully with divers and other disorderly persons to ayde them in their lewd, wicked and unlawful purpose'. Their aim appears to be defending their ancient commoners' rights from enclosure. Instead of settling this dispute in the local manor court, Hoddesdon attempted to intimidate his tenants by referring the case to the Star Chamber in London, run by men like himself who could be expected to be sympathetic. The case dragged on for years. A deal was eventually done and in exchange for land elsewhere the tenants stopped ripping down the fences.

Hoddesdon appears to have mellowed in his later years and, following the death of his first wife in 1602, married a young widow and was knighted by James I in 1603. He continued to live in the town until his death in February 1611 when he had a magnificent funeral, complete with heralds, and was buried in All Saints. His inscribed coffin lid is displayed on the south transept of the church along with that of his first wife Alice.

Christopher's only son, Francis, died as a child and his daughter, Ursula, became his heir. She married Sir John Leigh, the son of another city merchant family, but then died herself in 1595 while giving birth to a son. It was this boy, Thomas Leigh, who inherited the Leighton Buzzard manor in 1611, at the age of 16, when his grandfather Sir Christopher died.

The Leigh family continued to lease the manor from the Dean and Canons of Windsor

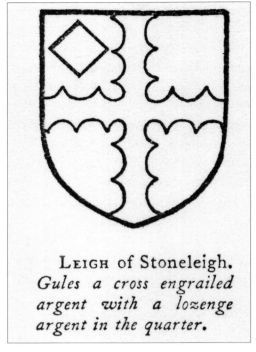

LEIGH of Stoneleigh.
Gules a cross engrailed argent with a lozenge argent in the quarter.

58 *The arms of the Leigh family who inherited the manor of Leighton Buzzard in 1611 and remained lords of the manor until the mid-19th century. Their coat of arms is still displayed on the front of the Victorian town hall in Market Square.*

and were to remain lords of Leighton until the middle of the 19th century.

Like most of the rest of England, both Leighton and Linslade continued as mixed agricultural estates. As can be seen from the battles Christopher Hoddesdon had with his tenants, the attitude of the lord of the manor mattered a great deal to everyone's welfare. From the mid-16th century it is possible for the lives of these ordinary families to be plotted by historians because records of baptisms, marriages and burials were kept for the first time.

In Linslade, after Elizabeth Hopton, who had built St Mary's Church tower, died in 1498 the heir was her son by her first marriage, Richard Corbet. The Corbets remained lords of this smaller manor across the river from Leighton for another 320 years. Although the family seat was Moreton Corbet in Shropshire, the Corbets frequently visited Linslade, possibly because of its proximity to London and the royal court. In 1538 Sir Roger Corbet, son of Richard, died at Linslade and directed in his will that he should be buried in St Mary's. His widow, Anne, survived for a further 13 years and took a close interest in the estate and lived in the manor house, the one that can still be seen next to the church today. Although the front of this house was rebuilt in the 'modern style' by an 18th-century Corbet, the cellars and roof timbers show the building was essentially the same one that Anne occupied in the 16th century.

60 *The Corbet raven in stone, now displayed on the front of Linslade Manor. It was originally on the wall of the older kitchen range at the rear of the house and shows the lord of the manor's motto 'Deus Pascit Corvos', which translates as 'God feeds the ravens'.*

CORBET. *Or a raven sable.*

59 *The black raven of the Corbet family's coat of arms. Again this is a word play on their name, 'Corbie' being the old French for a crow. They were lords of the manor at Linslade but their main seat was at Moreton Corbet in Shropshire.*

Some of the buildings in Leighton also date from this time. *The Peacock Inn*, no longer a pub, originally faced onto an open market and was not tucked behind the row of shops that now block the view down the High Street. This 'infilling' of the market place with a new row of shops reflects the increasing prosperity of the town. The Hall of the suppressed Fraternity took on a new lease of life as the *Cross Keys Inn*. The building survived until 1899, when it burnt down and was replaced by a brick building, at first an inn of the same name but now a bank. Some of the shops in the High Street, although subsequently modernised, also have Tudor timbering. The thatched cottages at Southcott in Linslade also date from this period.

Leighton remained through these changes a thriving market town, but life could be hard and the frequent return of the plague was a constant fear. A graphic example is a 'spoken will' of 1604 from the deathbed of Christopher Burton, who was dying of the plague. Almost every member of his family was wiped out by this highly contagious disease and so an

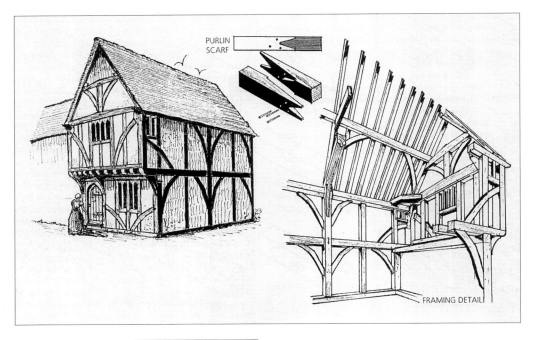

PURLIN
SCARF

FRAMING DETAIL

61 (Above) A reconstruction by John Bailey of the original timber-framing of The Peacock Inn. The method of construction dates the building to the early 15th century.

62 (Left) This old photograph of The Peacock Inn shows the building when it was still an inn. When built it had a prime position facing onto the wide market place. The ironwork, which originally held the inn sign, is still in situ.

inquiry into the circumstances of his will had to be made and witnesses called. From their statements we gain an insight into the fear and horror that the plague caused. Witnesses testified that Burton spoke to a relative who stood at the window 'but durst not come into the chamber for feare of ye sickness'. Burton told the relative that he gave all his goods to his wife and children and if they also died to any further relative that might survive. Burton died the following day.

The next major national event which must have dramatically affected life in Leighton and Linslade was the Civil War that began in 1642. Both the Leigh and Corbet families, along with the Dormers who owned Wing, supported the King against Cromwell and the Puritans. The Parliamentary forces controlled Aylesbury and Newport Pagnell, however. There are no battles recorded in the immediate area but forces from both sides must have pillaged the town for supplies. In 1644, for example, 10,000 Roundheads and their horses were billeted in Dunstable and Leighton Buzzard and in the same year King Charles I stayed at Ascott House in Wing.

A year later a major disaster overtook Leighton but details are scant and the cause unknown so it may have just been coincidence that fire destroyed many of the timber and thatched buildings of the High Street during the Civil War. A petition from 'the distressed inhabitants of Leighton Buzzard' to Parliament says

> By a fire which happened on 7th of March last, great damage was done to buildings and property in the town, amounting to £14,368 17s. Petitioners, who have been forward in all payments for Parliament, and have in consequence been mercilessly plundered by the enemy, pray that the House will grant them a collection in London and elsewhere for their relief.

Their request was ignored but the residents of Leighton were clearly resilient; a document of 1682 records a new building erected since 'the late miserable fire in Leighton' had destroyed the previous one. There is also a will of 1683

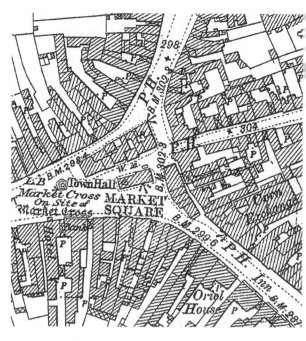

63 *Part of the 1901 Ordnance Survey map clearly showing the triangular shape and size of the original market place. The three blocks of buildings infilling part of this vast market are still the same shape and include the old town hall and two separate rows of shops, some of them built as early as the 16th century.*

64 *Holly Cottage facing Coopers Farmhouse, Southcott, a building which was once three cottages. The photograph, taken in the 19th century, is by one of the Leighton photographers, William and Theo Piggott, who used the cottage as a backdrop for a scene in one of their magic lantern shows.*

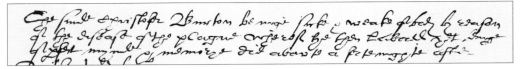

65 An extract from the 1604 plague will of Christopher Burton of Leighton Buzzard. It says, 'The saide Christofer Burton beinge sicke & weake of body by reason of the disease of the plague wherof he then lobored yet beinge of p[er]fect mynde & memorye did … make this will.'

from Thomas Meriden, the landlord of the *Raven*, an inn at 31-3 High Street, who leaves money for 'twelve good Sufficient Lether Fire Buckets [to] be hanged up under Leighton Bellofte neare my seat in the said church of Leighton Buzzard'.

The Leighs, Corbets, Dormers and the Verney family of Claydon in Buckinghamshire were all to see their estates sequestered by Parliament for their loyalty to the Royalist cause in the years following the execution of the King in 1649. Financial ruin ensued but the triumphant return of the Stuart dynasty in the form of Charles II in 1660 restored their estates and some of their fortunes.

One of the Corbet family, Sir Vincent, who had been dispossessed by Cromwell's men and died in poverty in London during the Commonwealth, had his family's sacrifice recognised when his widow, Sarah, was created Viscountess Linslade for her life. This is the only time the name of Leighton Buzzard or Linslade has been used as a title by a member of the nobility.

The upheaval of the Civil War meant loyalties had been divided, families split and in Leighton much property destroyed. The Restoration meant the people of the district could again begin to rebuild their lives and prosperity.

66 A painting of the Prebendal House by an artist called Orme, dated 1797. There is no record of its demolition after the last recorded tenant John Dickenson left in 1809 but it does not appear on Bevan's map of 1819. The cellar of the house still exists under the north-west corner of All Saints churchyard and until the Second World War young choirboys were 'dared' to face the 'devils' down the cellar steps.

6

Commodious Inns, Taxes and Gambling

The rebuilding of Leighton's prosperity began with the restoration of the manor to the Leigh family who had held it on a long lease from the Dean and Canons of Windsor before the Civil War. The manor had fallen into the hands of Colonel John Okey, a Roundhead who had been a judge at the trial of King Charles I and was the sixth among 60 Parliamentarians who had signed the death warrant in 1649.

Okey, described in a petition for the return of the lease as one of the murderers of the late King and a traitor, paid the price for regicide and was executed in 1662, two years after the restoration of Charles II to the throne. Thomas, Lord Leigh, gained the King's support for the return of the lease as 'a person of eminent loyalty'.

The Restoration also brought back the normal machinery of government and in 1662 a new tax, the Hearth Tax, was imposed to raise money for the running of the country. It was paid by those who could afford to heat their rooms. Every house, inn, dwelling or lodging had to pay 'for every firehearth or stove the sum of two shillings by the year'.

Linslade's returns for this date, which are no longer fully decipherable, show the largest house, with 16 hearths, was occupied by the lord of the manor Sir Vincent Corbet. This is the same house that stands next to St Mary's Church today. There are 23 households listed, indicating a total population of only 100 for the once thriving village. The next largest house, with five hearths, belonged to Robert Turney – a house that has since disappeared. The curate, the Rev. William Vaughan, had a house with three hearths but according to contemporary bishop's records this was a mile from the church. Sir Vincent was accused of pulling down the original vicarage and enclosing the garden and part of the churchyard in his parkland.

Complete tax documents for Leighton Buzzard for a slightly later return of 1671 give a picture of the town and the surrounding villages by listing every resident and the number of hearths on which he or she had to pay tax. The population of the town was 1,113 in 1671. Heath and Reach had a population of 323, Billington, 132, Eggington and

67   Linslade Manor House was home to the Corbets when they visited Linslade and their other Buckinghamshire estates from 1500 until around 1820. Refronted in the Georgian period it retains timbers from the earlier house.

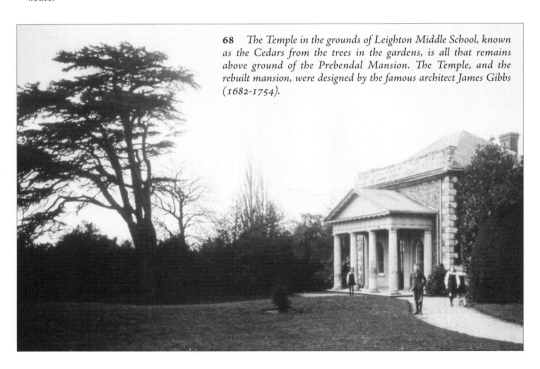

68   The Temple in the grounds of Leighton Middle School, known as the Cedars from the trees in the gardens, is all that remains above ground of the Prebendal Mansion. The Temple, and the rebuilt mansion, were designed by the famous architect James Gibbs (1682-1754).

Clipstone, 115, and Stanbridge, 234. The biggest house in Leighton had 16 hearths, which means 16 heated rooms, and was the Prebendal House. This was the home of Francis Winton, gentleman, a tenant of Leigh's. This grand house was originally built around the time of Domesday to accommodate the Bishop of Lincoln's official representative in the town, known as the prebend. The prebend's original job was to run the Bishop's Leighton estate, but direct running of the estate by the prebend had long ceased and the Leigh family leased it along with the rest of Leighton. Later the Leigh family came to live in the house themselves and rebuilt it in a grand manner. The last vestige of this once great house is the building known as The Temple, now in the grounds of Leighton Middle School. The rest was demolished around 1809.

The next two big Hearth Tax payers of 1671 are the landlords of the two big inns, *The Bell* and the *Swan* on the Market Square, which were still serving customers on the same sites in 2008. Daniel Hinton, landlord at *The Bell*, paid tax on 11 hearths and John Walker at the *Swan* paid on ten.

The importance of inns in the life of the town is illustrated by the large number of them and by the fact that, apart from the Prebendal Manor, all the big Hearth Tax payers are publicans. On the north side of the High Street, on the site of the National Westminster bank, was the *Red Lion* where William Maulcott also paid tax for 10 hearths. This large inn was, extraordinarily, one of five hostelries that stood in a row on that side of the High Street. On one side of the *Red Lion* was the *Cock* with six hearths, the *Raven* with eight hearths and the *Mermaid* with four hearths, and on the other side the *Black Lion* with three hearths. The landlord of the *Raven* was the same Thomas Meriden who was mentioned in the last chapter as giving 12 good fire buckets to be hung in the church. Further up the High Street was the *Saracen's Head* with four hearths and the *Eagle & Child*, opposite the Market Cross, with six hearths.

The vast majority of ordinary households in Leighton Buzzard had just one hearth, or heated room, and even the better-off inhabitants had only two, with a few having

69 The Bell *public house, in a prime position in the market place, was first recorded in the 1490s during the reign of Henry VII and was once owned by the Wilkes family, who provided the almshouses.*

70, 71 *(Left and below) The Swan public house was one of Leighton's great coaching inns, dating from 1600 but refronted in the early 19th century. The balcony over the ornate porch was often used to address public meetings and Francis Bassett thanked the voters of Leighton Buzzard from here when elected MP for Bedfordshire in 1872. The balcony also provided a view of the traditional Boxing Day hunt in the town. The scene outside the Swan is recorded in the photograph below taken around 1910.*

72 *(Opposite) The Wilkes Almshouses in North Street were originally built in 1630. They were restored and enlarged by the Victorians reusing some original stonework.*

73 *(Below Right) A section of the 1880 Ordnance Survey Town Plan showing the internal layout of both the Wilkes Almshouses and the Friends Meeting House in North Street.*

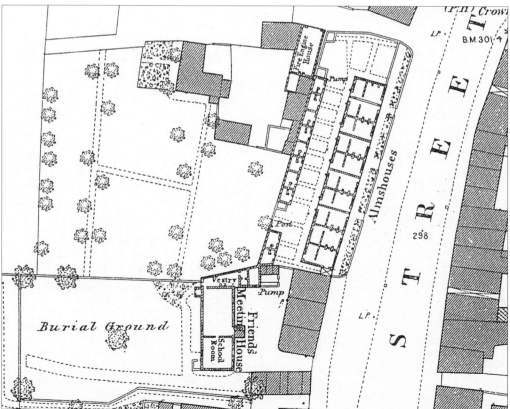

more. Seventy householders were 'discharged by certificate' as being too poor to pay the tax. This included the occupants of eight Wilkes Charity almshouses in North Street, occupied by widows. This charity had originally been set up in 1630 by Edward Wilkes, a merchant, and subsequently added to by other members of the family.

Each of the villages also had a big house, and Heath and Reach had two, reflecting the fact that it was formerly two villages. Heath House, occupied by Mr Vaux, had 11 hearths. The house is still there opposite St Leonard's Church. At Reach there was a huge house with 14 hearths, since disappeared. Twenty-six households were exempt from the tax in the two settlements.

Billington paid tax on a total of 68 hearths and had three larger houses with five or six hearths, four almshouses (now disappeared), but surprisingly no poor listed in the village. Eggington and Clipstone were counted together in the tax return, with five people being supported by charity and one large house with six hearths. Stanbridge is a substantial village with 77 taxed hearths. There is no great house but five substantial farmhouses with four hearths each and one with five. Four heads of household were exempt from the tax through poverty and

a further 13 people who were in 'receipt of constant alms' also did not have to pay.

Another insight into life after the Restoration is also provided by the Hearth Tax. Trade tokens were used at the time instead of money by local shops because coins were in short supply. Five tokens issued by traders listed in the Hearth Tax of 1671 still survive. Among them are those of Benedict Coles, a grocer, who had three hearths and a shop next to the *Saracen's Head* on the High Street, and Isaac Hannell, who had a half-penny token showing two pipes and a roll of tobacco and the date 1667. He is listed in the

74 *A half-penny token dating from 1667 issued by a High Street grocer, Benedict Coles, when coinage was scarce following the restoration of the monarchy. On one side is the name 'Layton' and the date and in the centre 'his half peny'. On the reverse is a pair of scales denoting his trade as a grocer and his name. Coles' shop was on the north side of the High Street near the Market Cross. This is one of five surviving types of Leighton Buzzard traders' tokens.*

75 *The east side of Lake Street about 1880 showing the splendid Corn Exchange and other buildings, all of which are much earlier. The corn market was held at the top end of Lake Street and horse market lower down, sights familiar to the diarist John Salusbury.*

Hearth Tax with three hearths, living close to the *Swan* on the Market Square. This is less than a century after Walter Raleigh discovered natives smoking in America and shows how quickly this new fashion had spread.

The size of the inns in Leighton Buzzard in 1671 shows how central they were to the life of the town. There were no banks, post offices, solicitors, restaurants or cafes, but all business was transacted in inns and taverns. The roads were also terrible so travel on coaches and by horseback was slow. Stagecoaches had to change their teams of horses every 10 to 15 miles and the *Swan* in Leighton provided those new teams as the passengers took a break in their journey.

Inns were also central on market and fair days. Markets were held twice a week. The main market was on Tuesday when the town would be full of farmers and traders selling farm produce and the inns would have been packed with people doing business. Almost to the end of the 20th century Leighton Buzzard was renowned for 'tiddly Tuesday', when red-faced farmers spent all day in the pubs, which were licensed all day.

The pubs and the market of this period were also frequented by rogues and pickpockets. One recorded example from a Tuesday market day, 4 September 1677, describes Lawrence Cripps, a Ridgmont butcher, haggling for an hour with Joseph Warner who was trying to sell him three 'steares'. The cattle were turned into the yard behind the *Swan* while the two men bargained in the tap room inside. The deal was never completed because the man who collected the market tolls arrested Warner as a suspected cattle rustler, an offence that carried the death penalty.

76 *The Maidenhead, on the west side of Lake Street, was the home of John Salusbury. The pub was first mentioned in the will of Thomas Keyser. He had emigrated from Leighton to Jamaica and died there, leaving his property to his daughters. They had married sugar planters whose estates were run by slave labour. The building was demolished in 1956.*

Perhaps the most important trading days of the year were the fairs. These varied over the centuries but charters for six fairs for Leighton exist altogether. For example, in 1630, Sir Thomas Leigh was granted a charter by the King to hold St Paul's Fair on 25 January each year. He was also granted a 'Cherry Fair' to be held on 15 July. Fairs brought hundreds of people to the town to buy horses, wool and other commodities.

For those out of work the most important fair of the year was Michaelmas at the end of September. The statute or 'Statty' fair was held in the High Street. Men and women seeking work would stand outside the *Swan* advertising their trade by wearing symbols on their clothes. For example, shepherds had wool through a buttonhole, cowmen had cowhair and horsekeepers had whipcord. On receiving a shilling they were engaged for a year. This practice was referred to by John Salusbury, Esquire, described as a gentleman, who lived in a fine house in Lake Street. His diary, for which two years of daily entries covering 1757-9 survive, gives a fascinating picture of

life in the town. A bachelor, Salusbury, was a pillar of local society, a magistrate, an officer and secretary of the Bedfordshire Militia, and a tax commissioner, but also a gambler and drinker. He had a pet dog, Flora, who he records 'pupped' three times in two years.

The importance of the fairs to Leighton are clear in his diary, not least because he rented out the railings in front of his house to various traders from as far away as Northampton. His home had once been the *Maidenhead Inn* and must have had an imposing frontage because he let out the left-hand rails to one trader, the right-hand to another, and on busy days the gateway to a third, charging them each rent for the privilege. On a fair day of 24 October 1757 he records, 'Goodman paid me for my left hand rails, but Bennett did not for those on the right, let my gateway to one Whitbread of Eversholt for one shilling and six pence.' He later caught up with Bennett and obtained his 10s. rent for the rails for three fairs. From the entries and other evidence it seems the rails were used by traders for tying up horses for sale.

The size of Salusbury's house can only be guessed at. By this time the unpopular Hearth Tax had been replaced by a Window Tax which was paid by houses with more than seven windows and increased if you had more than nine. Salusbury's house stood opposite the current library in Lake Street and he records paying window tax for '37 lights'. Salusbury's income came from property he owned in Leighton Buzzard, including the *Unicorn Inn*, and houses in Eggington to which he refers because constant repairs are requested by the tenants.

Salusbury was a keen gardener and records the times he plants and harvests artichokes, asparagus, beans, including kidney and dwarf beans, broccoli, cabbages, carrots, cauliflower, celery, onions, parsley and peas. There were five sorts of apples and Burgundy pears. He also had vines but does not record whether he made wine. The only flowers he mentions are tulips and hollyhocks.

Salusbury acquires malting barley to make ale and a particular strong beer called nappy. He records drinking cider, raisin wine, port, punch, rumbo (which is rum) and shrub, a drink still found in the West Country. He had particular friends, whom he met two or three times a week, and most days, especially when in the company of ladies, drank tea. Tea drinking was at the height of fashion in this period and was very expensive. He records the gift of a teapot from a lady friend in London and paying 5s. for half a pound of green tea and on the same day 3s. 8d. for eight chickens.

Food is not so frequently mentioned as drink and gambling but Salusbury buys a

pike from people dragging the pond at Heath and Reach, has barrels of oysters sent up from London and is given a haunch of venison by the Duke of Bedford. For one dinner party

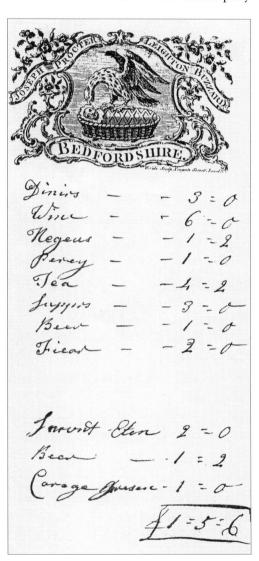

77 *A bill dating from the 1770s from the* Eagle & Child *coaching inn, in Market Square. The bill includes six shillings for wine and one shilling for beer and 1s. 2d. for negus, a hot toddy of port, lemon, sugar and spices. Included on the bill is two shillings for fuel for the fire and one shilling for stabling horses.*

for six friends on a fair day he gives the menu: 'Green pease soup, three boiled chickens, bacon, hunting pudding, two roast ducks, neck of veal, pease, tarts, and custard'.

John Salusbury wore a wig and travelled about mostly on his horse to visit friends in neighbouring towns and villages, although he also travelled by carriage and frequently walked long distances. Many of the visits involved dining and drinking and two or three nights a week he stayed with his hosts, returning home after breakfast the following day. When he entertained, in return, his guests also 'lay the night'.

The welfare, feeding and shoeing of Salusbury's horse are carefully recorded, including the practice of banging nails into the horses hooves in order to ride in heavy frost – a forerunner of chains on wheeled vehicles to deal with snow.

He belonged to the Civil Society, a gentlemen's club of around twenty prominent citizens that met in various inns and taverns at the nomination of one of the members, who played cards and backgammon for money and discussed the affairs of the day. He also

attended dances at the *Swan* where on one occasion he took several dances with Mrs Townsend and Mrs Ward (his friends' wives) and lost six pence at a game of cards called quadrille. His party broke up at 2 a.m. but the other revellers continued until 6 a.m. He comments, 'There were eleven gentlemen and it cost us 6 shillings 6 pence apiece.'

He also records attending a number of plays at the Town Hall in Leighton's Market Square including Shakespeare's *Richard III*.

Salusbury knew all the gentry in the county and records going to Woburn to watch a series of cricket matches and making bets on the outcome. He wins and loses several bets before totalling up a surplus of 7s. 6d. over three days of matches. There were also race meetings to attend in Bedford, Aylesbury and on one occasion in King's Mead, the name of a large field in the water meadows below All Saints, Leighton Buzzard. He records on 14 October 1758, 'There was a race in King's Mead for a purse of £3, (and) a saddle and a foot race for a smock.'

Apart from his servants, ordinary citizens of Leighton Buzzard, other than tradesmen

78 *Holly Lodge, a large Jacobean House, was built in the early 17th century and jutted out into North Street. It was a fine old house, which fell into decay and was used as a potato store in the 1950s before being demolished to make way for West Street.*

and criminals, rarely get a mention, although in his role as a magistrate he officiates over legal documents binding new apprentices to their trade. He mentions a young child dying of smallpox, and when taking on a servant called William Gilbert comments that the lad has not had the disease and 'if he should fall (ill) in my service he is to be at his own expense'.

His duties as a magistrate took him to Bedford Assizes where he says that in one day four people were tried and sentenced to death – two for a burglary, one for horse stealing and the fourth for sheep stealing.

While Salusbury eats and dines well and frequently records tipping servants, there are clearly poor people in the town who find life hard. One entry for 12 September 1759 says: 'A great disturbance and noise among the poor people in the town today on account of the farmers having prohibited them from raking haum in the fields.' Haum, or haulm, is the stalks of corn, beans and other crops left after harvest which could be used for bedding or even fuel. Salusbury's diary is sadly lost after this date, but he continued to live in Leighton and died in the summer of 1787. In his will he left money and property to his servant, Mary Crawley, including 'a shop and chamber adjacent to *The Bell Inn*'.

Two years before Salusbury died, the 1785 directory for Bedfordshire describes Leighton as 'A pleasant and populous town, agreeably situated on a branch of the Ouse, and rendered flourishing by a good trade and large markets. The houses in general well built, and diversified, with some handsome ones, and commodious inns.' It gives a list of tradespeople which

79 *A Leighton Buzzard entry from a trade directory of 1785 giving details of the town's commercial life and its tradesmen. Among them is William Claridge, who ran wagons to London from the Unicorn Inn in Lake Street. He was the tenant of Leighton diarist John Salusbury, who was a near neighbour.*

includes two attorneys at law, three surgeons, three butchers, five drapers, two grocers, four maltsters, a basket maker, a breeches-maker and glover and a watchmaker. The presence

80 *The Friends Meeting House is set back behind the houses in North Street with its own archway entrance onto the main road. It was built in 1789 by the local Quaker community which included many of the town shopkeepers and craftsmen.*

of two lace dealers gives a clue to one of the cottage industries in the town. There are three insurance agents mentioned and other trades like ironmonger, glazier and plumber, carpenter and joiner. Two woolstaplers, who grade and sell on large quantities of wool are also in business in the town.

The directory says there is a wagon service to London on Tuesdays and Thursdays from Leighton Buzzard to the *Cross Keys* in St John Street in the City.

Five regular fairs are listed in 1785, 'being on February 24, the Tuesday before Easter, Whit Tuesday, July 26 and October 24'.

The directory is a snapshot of Leighton Buzzard just before the industrial revolution. The town was clearly already changing because alongside the description of All Saints as a 'good church' is mention of a 'neat meeting house belonging to the dissenters'. This is believed to be a reference to the first Baptist Chapel built less than 10 years earlier. These 'dissenters' baptised people in the River Ouzel but there were already other breakaway Christian denominations. Two years after the directory was published the Quaker Meeting House, behind the Almshouses in North

Street, was completed to accommodate a growing congregation. Among the leading Quakers was Peter Bassett, one of the town's drapers mentioned in the 1785 directory. He was a member of a family that was to play a key role in the life of the town in the following century. Another Quaker in the directory is Joseph Brooks, a woolstapler.

Although many of the features and traditions of Leighton Buzzard would remain unchanged in the 19th century, especially the markets and reliance on agriculture, much else altered with the industrial revolution. On the other side of the River Ouzel in Linslade these changes were dramatic.

The village had continued to decline and in 1740 Corbet Kynaston, who had inherited the manor through his mother, Beatrice Corbet, went spectacularly bankrupt and 18 farms in Linslade had to be sold to pay his debts. Another branch of the family managed to retain the manor house and some land but were forced to rent it out.

But a new era was beginning for Linslade. First the canal and then the railway arrived, stimulating the building of a new town and rapid growth in population.

7
Boats, Turnpikes and Trains

Some of the farmers who had bought chunks of the bankrupt Corbet estate in Linslade would have been among an excited crowd who attended a meeting in Stony Stratford in 1792 hoping to invest in a proposed London to Birmingham canal.

The meeting was originally to have been in the *Red Lion* at Stony Stratford but had to be transferred to the parish church because of the large number of people wanting to attend. The idea of a new canal was so popular because those built in the north of England since 1750 were making large profits for investors. They had opened new trade routes and promoted industrial development along the banks.

Some of these new owners of single farms in Linslade were no doubt among investors who swapped land through which the canal would be built for shares in the new canal company. The route the canal took was through fields owned by many farmers, making them easier to bargain with than single powerful estate owners. In some places the courses of canals and railways had to be altered because of objections from large landowners. In Linslade

the opposite appears to have been the case; the canal was welcomed.

An Act of Parliament authorising the Grand Junction Canal, as it was then called, was passed in April 1793 and work began a month later. Thousands of people were employed on the project, which was dug by hand, and labourers came from as far away as Scotland, Wales and Ireland. These men, called 'navvies' because they worked on the navigation, brought their families with them and lived in temporary encampments next to the canal as work moved forward.

The colossal project, costing £361,000, progressed with remarkable speed and the first loaded barge arrived in Linslade on 28 May 1800. John Dickenson, a country gentleman who rented the Prebendal House in Leighton between 1797 and 1809, records in his diary, 'The canal was opened today and several barges with coal arrived.' These barges, the same design as today's narrowboats but horse drawn, carried 30 tons of coal. This was a vast payload compared with the only other means of transport at the time, a horse-drawn

81   *The Bedford Arms, Linslade, on the right, was first licensed in 1800 when the canal opened and was called the Corbet Arms. The building itself is timber-framed and dates from before this but there is no record of its use before it became a pub. The corner shop on the left has been demolished and the war memorial re-sited in Mentmore Road Memorial Gardens.*

wagon. Coal had previously been a luxury brought by sea, then up the Ouse to Bedford, the limit of the river navigation, and finally by wagon along the appalling roads of the period.

The opening of the canal began to transform Linslade. It shifted the focus of the town from the old manor and St Mary's Church to the new wharves built along the canal next to the main road from Aylesbury into Leighton.

The *Bedford Arms*, next to the bridge, where some of the horses used for towing barges were stabled, dates from this time. Its licence was

granted in 1800. Apart from adding a new public house, the opening of the canal made an immediate difference to the commercial life and prosperity of Leighton. For example, John Grant, a prominent Quaker who farmed in Linslade and had a grocery business in North Street, went into partnership with two others, William Exton and Edward Lawford, as corn, coal and timber merchants and 'wharfingers'. What is labelled on Victorian maps as Grant's wharf was one of three new unloading and turning places on the canal intended for trade. Grant and his partners built their wharf on

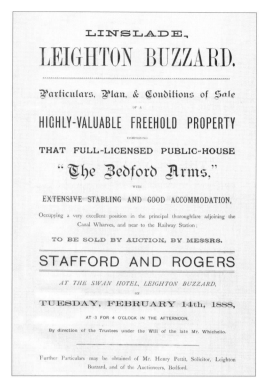

82 *An 1888 poster announcing the impending sale of the Bedford Arms following the death of its owner, wealthy woolstapler Stephen Whichello, who gave his name to the wharf behind the pub. He lived in The Elms on Stoke Road. The stabling was for horses for working canal barges.*

the Leighton side of the bridge, with its own basin. The basin silted up and is now filled in but the bridge they built over it to carry the towpath and the horses which pulled the barges remains, as does their headquarters, Grand Union House in Bridge Street. Early directories for Leighton Buzzard reflect the increase in trade. The 1785 directory lists 15 merchants and tradesmen for Leighton Buzzard but the 1811 version has 58.

Among those listed in the directories was a civil engineer, Benjamin Bevan. He was originally a surveyor and was appointed engineer to the middle district of the Grand

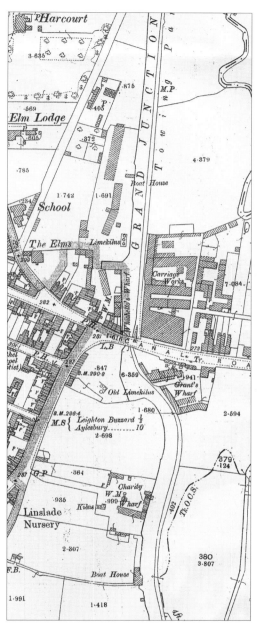

83 *An extract from the 1901 Ordnance Survey map showing the wharves on the Grand Junction Canal. They are Whichello's wharf, north of the bridge, and, to the south, Grant's Wharf on the east side and Charity Wharf on the west. The first two wharves get their names from their owners but the last reflects the fact that the field in which it stood was owned by the Wilkes Charity. There were two more wharves at Old Linslade.*

Junction Canal in 1805. He lived at the bottom of the High Street facing Church Square. Bevan was famous in his day for inventing the slide rule and, among other talents, was an astronomer.

Bevan saved the canal from a catastrophic technical failure in 1808. He had predicted that the Wolverton section of the canal over the River Ouse would fail. The aqueduct duly collapsed and Bevan was charged with supervising its replacement and suggested a giant cast-iron trough large enough for two narrow boats to pass – a radical solution at the time since cast iron was still a new technology. 'The iron trunk' was installed by 1811 and still carries the canal. A plaque at the site commemorates this engineering feat.

Bevan died in 1833 while viewing an eclipse of the moon from the window of his High Street house. He left all his papers, manuscripts and mathematical instruments to his son, also called Benjamin, who had followed his father as a surveyor and drew the first detailed map of the town in 1819.

Another prominent citizen recorded in the 1811 directory was Charles Pettit, who was lace manufacturer to HRH Princess Charlotte of Wales, the daughter of the Prince Regent, later George IV. At the time Leighton was a centre for lace making and straw plait manufacturing, mainly for hats and bonnets.

Among the services offered by the canal were 'fly boats'. The 1830 directory advertises 'Conveyance by water to London, Birmingham, Manchester etc fly boats pass daily, by which goods left at the wharfs of Messrs Grant and Lawford, J. Osborne, and John Young, are safely forwarded to all parts of the kingdom.'

But the major difference the canal made was the ability to carry bulk cargoes. Up to this time Leighton's sand industry had been providing material locally, within a radius of about twenty miles, but the canal meant that many tons of sand could be delivered easily to massive building projects in London and the Midlands as well as providing raw materials for industries.

The coal barges coming from the Midlands pits meant local businessmen were able to open the Leighton Buzzard Gas and Coke Company. This was formed in 1835 when pipes were laid

84 *A barge at Brantom's Wharf, earlier called Grant's Wharf, in 1928. The barge is loading wheat for delivery to London. The two Leighton workers are A. Holmes and A. Barton. This loading dock has been filled in but the bridge which carried the towpath over it remains.*

85 *A drawing of Wharf Cottages on Charity Wharf by local historian Frederick Gurney. He drew this in 1919 and notes that the cottages were demolished in 1926. The site now houses several blocks of flats called The Wharf.*

up Lake Street, High Street, North Street and Hockliffe Street and 32 houses and some street lamps were connected within a year. Coal was heated in retorts and the gas extracted on a site at the corner of Stanbridge Road and Billington Road. The gas was held in giant holders to ensure a regular supply and the porous lumps of coke left after the heating process were sold on as a poor quality but smokeless fuel.

Gas cookers and fires could be hired from the company at 9d. a quarter and the new gas mantles meant shopkeepers could illuminate their wares without having to rely on oil lamps and candles.

Although goods of all kinds were being carried on the canal people still relied on the roads for transport. Regular coach services

had run on England's roads since the 1650s, but not through Leighton Buzzard. This was partly because there was little demand but mainly owing to the poor state of the roads. People who wanted to travel hired a post-chaise from one of the inns like the *Swan* or *Eagle & Child* and travelled to Hockliffe to catch the stagecoach, which ran along Watling Street to London or the North West. This road, originally built by the Romans, was kept in good repair because travellers paid a toll to use it, collected at intervals along the route. In the 18th century John Salusbury, whose

86 *The new enlarged gasworks was built in 1882 in Grovebury Road, next to the Dunstable branch railway line, so coal could be brought direct from the mines in 10 ton railway trucks. This took the trade from the canals that had serviced the old gasworks at the corner of Billington Road and Stanbridge Road.*

87 *The new town of Linslade attracted new industries, in this case coach building. This is an advert in the trade directory of 1877 for George King, manufacturer of coaches, who proudly displays the fact that he has patented his own designs.*

the country. The section from Dunstable northwards was widened and maintained using surplus sandstone dug up in Leighton pits. A turnpike was originally a frame set with spikes to prevent passage until the toll was paid, but was later replaced with gates.

The state of the main road was so bad that in 1810 Assize judges travelling round the country to dispense justice made a large detour to avoid Leighton. Those travelling from the court at Aylesbury to Bedford went in a large loop via Berkhamsted to get to Hockliffe rather than face Linslade and Leighton Buzzard roads. That year a turnpike was agreed from Aylesbury to Hockliffe, via

diary was discussed in the previous chapter, records attending meetings in Dunstable as a commissioner of this turnpike, the first in

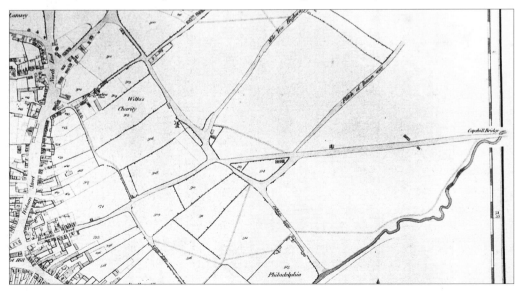

88 *The eastern part of the 1819 Bevan map shows the new toll road created in 1810 cutting diagonally across the existing road layout and the open fields. This route replaced the old West Lane, which ran via Lake Street. As its name suggests, Lake Street was frequently flooded where it crossed the Clipstone Brook.*

Wing, crossing the canal and river at Linslade. It travelled up the High Street, turned right on Jeffes Lane, now Hockliffe Street, and continued to Eggington and Hockliffe. The aim was to upgrade the road from a muddy rutted track to a hard and smooth surface. A Bill dated 18 May 1810 set out the turnpike rules, including detailed tolls to be paid for various vehicles and maximum loads. There was a weighbridge and a record kept of tolls paid and for what size of vehicle. A maximum permitted vehicle weight was not to be exceeded for fear of damaging the road surface, but there were subsequent complaints that this rule had been flouted by allowing excess loads to pay double.

The Turnpike Trustees' surveyor regularly reported on the condition of the road and in December 1813 wrote

> I found the Hockliffe Parish on the said Road Very much cut through and in a bad state. Also the Eggington nearley in the same state.
>
> Leighton is in a passable state for the season except a short length on the lane called Jeffes Lane which is worn very much since my last survey.
>
> Linslade is much worn tho not daingerous for traveling.

The turnpike was not a universally popular idea and the people of Leighton objected to it, presumably on the grounds that paying tolls to reach the town might discourage people from visiting, and in particular attending the all-important markets and fairs. A compromise was reached by placing the tollgates well out of town at the edge of Linslade and Leighton parishes so local people at least would be exempt from charges.

The new road made possible regular stagecoach services from Leighton Buzzard to London and between Oxford and Cambridge. Details of these services are given in the 1830 *National Commercial Directory*, all leaving from or stopping at the *Swan* in the High Street. The London coach left the *Swan* every morning except Sunday, at 7 a.m., and went through Hockliffe, Dunstable and St Albans.

The Cambridge coach called at the *Swan* every Monday, Wednesday and Friday at 12 noon, and went through to Woburn, Ampthill, Bedford and St Neots. The same coach obviously went one way one day and returned the next because the Oxford coach called at the *Swan* on Tuesday, Thursday

89 *This is believed to be the coachman who for years ran the service between Oxford and Cambridge via the* Swan *posting house in Leighton Buzzard. It was a gruelling journey that took all day.*

and Saturday at 2 p.m. and went through Aylesbury.

Coaches had to stop for a change of horses every 10 to 12 miles to keep up an average speed of 12 miles per hour, and the *Swan* provided the horses and the stabling to do this. Changing horses could take as little as five minutes but the *Swan* stop, at least on the route to Cambridge, included half an hour for passengers to have lunch.

Travelling on coaches could be tough, inside passengers paying about two thirds more than those who rode on top. There was only room for four inside what was a small box with seats, with tiny windows for ventilation and view. Outside, however, there was the weather. It was not unknown for outside passengers to freeze to death or fall off, breaking bones and sometimes being run over by the coach's rear wheels. In the summer there was the dust from unmade roads. Sometimes, on steep hills or the worst roads, passengers might be required to dismount and keep up on foot. Coach fares from Leighton to London at this time are unknown but fares from the *Swan* at Bedford to London for a one way ticket was 12s. on the inside and 6s. and 6d. on the outside. There were costs also for excess baggage.

By 1830 Leighton and Linslade were clearly growing fast and enjoying new prosperity. A directory describes Leighton as 'a thriving and respectable market town' that

enjoys a considerable trade in corn, timber, seed, iron etc., the grand junction canal affording, by its proximity, the means of conveyance to all parts. There are also some very respectable establishments in the lime and brick trade; and the making of straw plat and lace (as in many other towns in the county) gives employment to a great number of females.

The population had also increased substantially. For example, in Linslade in 1798 only 43 able bodied men were recorded as being fit enough to fight, if needed, the French. The adjoining parish of Wing had six times as many. The full census of 1801, in which the government counted the entire population of the country for the first time, put the total of men, women and children in Linslade at 203. This was a year after the canal opened and the population doubled to 407 by 1831. Leighton's population in 1801 was 1,963, and was 3,330 some thirty years later.

Among the trades mentioned in the 1830 directory for Leighton Buzzard are 13 bakers, nine butchers, four grocers and four plumbers, painters and glaziers. There were also two boot and shoemakers, three dressmakers, four straw-hatmakers, four tailors and three hairdressers. Reflecting the importance of pubs in the town, a brewer, wine and spirit merchant, two inns and 25 taverns are recorded.

Sitting oddly in this directory of commercial activity is a reference to Leighton's religious dissenters: Quakers, Baptists and Methodists were flourishing in the town and surrounding villages where chapels were being built by public subscription. The directory says, 'The Quakers, who are a numerous and respectable class here, have a meeting house for their devotional exercises, as have the Baptists and Methodists.' A different view had been taken

90 *The Workhouse, Grovebury Road, Leighton was built in 1834 to house 100 men, 100 women and 50 children. Unlike many workhouses, which were turned into hospitals, this was later adapted for other purposes. After being requisitioned in the Second World War to house service personnel, the buildings were converted to offices.*

exception of Mr Wilson the curate and a few other friends as Church and King Men.'

The directory does not mention the town's poor at all although there were obviously quite large numbers of them. In 1834 the Poor Law Amendment Act was passed allowing groups of parishes in the district to combine into Unions to build workhouses for those unable to support themselves. Each parish had its own workhouse before this date, and Leighton's, in Baker Street, was overflowing. Four acres of land were bought to build a new workhouse in what is now Grovebury Road. This was completed in 1836, for 100 men and 100 women who were accommodated in separate dormitories. There were also facilities for 50 children. The building, which was used to house the poor for 100 years, is still standing and has been adapted for use as offices. Not much is known about conditions in Leighton Union workhouse but families were split up on arrival and only the desperate would willingly go there.

by Thomas Lane Wood, the steward, writing to James Leigh, the lord of the manor in 1821. He complained of being 'surrounded by Quakers, dissenters and radicals of the worst kind … I am almost alone with the

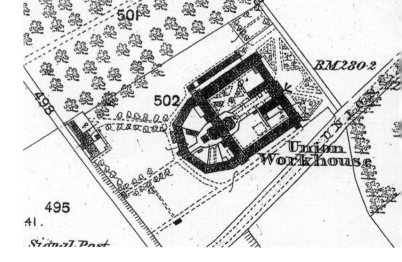

91 *The Workhouse as depicted on the 1901 Ordnance Survey map. The building has undergone many changes since but the core of the structure is the same as shown here.*

92 *The Globe Inn, Linslade. The building pre-dates the canal, and is still partly a barn in this early picture. It soon became a popular inn.*

The sexes were segregated in separate dining rooms, kitchens and work rooms.

The nonconformists, who rated a special mention in the directory, came to play an important role in Leighton life and made a major contribution to its prosperity, although at times their views and behaviour were controversial, as we shall see in the next chapter. One of the Quakers already mentioned was John Grant, who bought the old workhouse in Baker Street and turned it into rented rooms. Much of his wealth may have come from a major interest in the canal, particularly his wharf next to the main road into the town. It was not surprising, therefore, to find him objecting to the next phase of Leighton's development, the arrival of the railway.

93 *Breaking the ice on the Grand Junction Canal. The boat is rocked from side to side at the front to smash the ice. In the days of wooden-hulled boats the ice was a severe hazard, cutting into the barges as they moved forward. One of the boasts of the competing railway was that canal traffic was unreliable in the winter.*

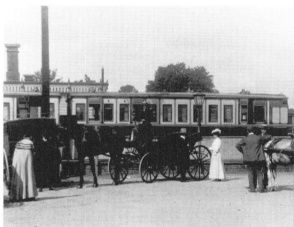

94-6 *These early pictures of the old Leighton Buzzard railway station were taken by one of the Piggott brothers and have only recently been discovered. One shows the station master talking to a small boy next to an advertisement for champagne, reflecting the hunting clientele from London who used the railway. Another picture shows carriages and carts meeting the train.*

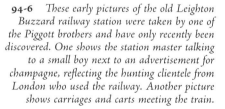

Both the turnpike trusts and shareholders in the canals opposed the arrival of railways so soon after they had made their own investments. They feared the competition. There was also opposition to the route proposed by the young engineer, Robert Stephenson. He wanted to put the railway between the canal and All Saints Church along the river valley. Among the objectors, besides Grant, was Lady Sarah Lovett of Liscombe Park, Soulbury. Both owned land affected by the proposed route of the railway and would not allow it to be used.

However, a public meeting in the town in 1831 was in favour of the proposed railway and a route was found going through Linslade. This required the London & Birmingham Railway Company to tunnel through Jackdaw Hill (now known as Tunnel Hill), something that would have been avoided on the original route. It also proved a costly decision for the railway because the hill was composed mainly of ironstone and was very difficult to tunnel through.

The construction of the line brought another influx of new people into the Leighton area.

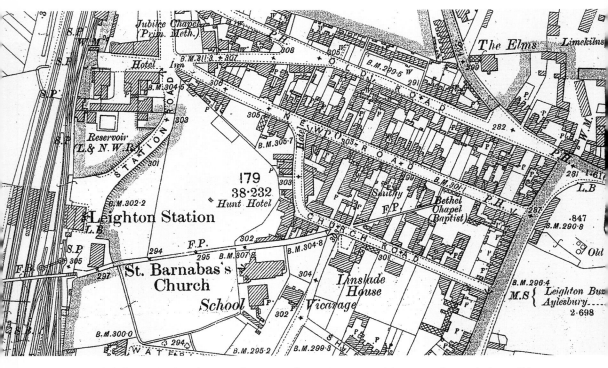

97 Linslade 'New Town' as shown on the 1901 Ordnance Survey map. The new roads were built parallel to the 'Old Road' and plots laid out for houses and shops. The old field footpaths across the area were retained in the design and still survive.

The original gangs of workmen being hired to build the railway were drawn from large numbers of unemployed itinerants, some of whom had roamed the country looking for work for years following the disbanding of the army at the end of the Napoleonic wars.

While the canal had begun the development of a new Linslade, the difference the railway made when it opened in 1838 was dramatic. It was constructed through green fields and the new station was between the road to Soulbury and the turnpike to Wing. Between these two roads, the station and the canal, a new town was laid out. The first road laid to the station in 1839 is still called New Road.

In Leighton, the first immediate effect of the railway was the loss of the stagecoach service to London, although the east-west Oxford-Cambridge service continued. The *Swan* now ran a shuttle service collecting people from the station.

The demand for coal led to one other new development. Coal for Dunstable had been brought to Leighton and transferred the last nine miles by road, but so great was the volume that a railway branch line from Leighton was built and opened in 1848.

Over a period of less than 40 years Leighton and Linslade had entered Britain's new industrial age.

8

Enclosure, Sand, Quakers and Hunting

The canal and railway brought the district into the industrial age, but Leighton in the 1830s still had a medieval three-field system of agriculture. In most of the country this communal system of farming, whereby tenants held strips of land within great open fields, had been swept away. In Leighton it had existed almost unchanged for about a thousand years. The lords of the manor owned the land but the tenants had rights to graze common land and, particularly in Leighton, rights to gather sandstone and sand from the heath for building, and brushwood for their fires.

In the rest of the country, including Linslade, these open fields and commons had been gradually enclosed over previous centuries to form modern farms. This had led to the creation of smaller hedged fields that were far more efficient. But moving from one system to another in one step, as was proposed in Leighton, was highly contentious because the poorest members of the community, farm labourers for example, lost all their commoners rights. These included the right to allow their animals, such as the family cow

or pig, onto the communal fields for grazing after the harvest. Using the common land for grazing or for gathering stone and wood to supplement meagre wages had allowed the poor to scratch a living for centuries. After enclosure these activities would be banned.

Acts of Parliament were required in 1836, 1840 and 1843 to change the face of the landscape around Leighton and its surrounding villages. Each village had its open three-field system turned into farms. The larger tenants, who had the most open field strips under the old system, got large and profitable farms, while smaller tenants got smallholdings and labourers were left virtually destitute. Some who could not find jobs ended up in Leighton's new workhouse.

Parliamentary Commissioners heard appeals against enclosure. In Leighton, petitioners who described themselves as 'small proprietors' said the enclosure would prove 'very injurious, detrimental and in many respects ruinous'. Witnesses gave evidence at the Town Hall about how they, and their fathers before them, had earned a living in lean times by digging

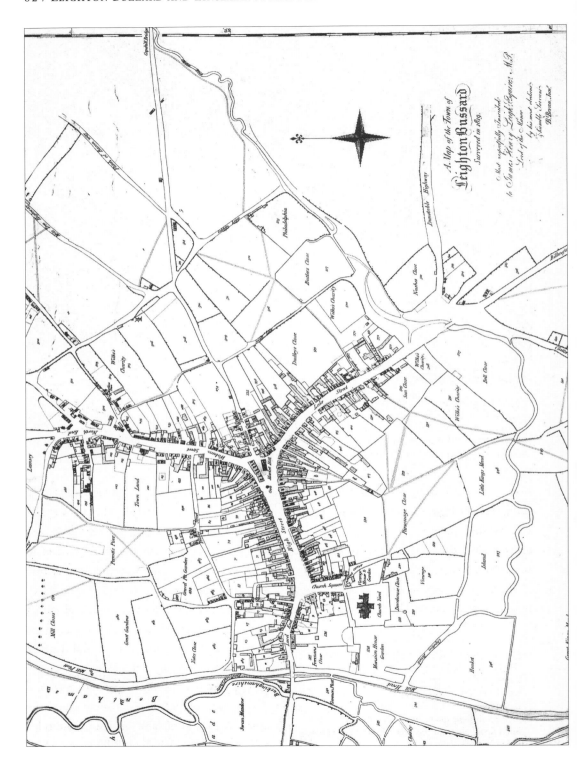

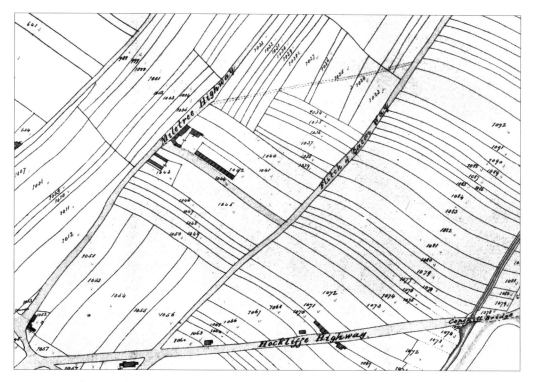

99 *A small section of the Leighton Buzzard Tithe Map of 1843. The strip system shown on the map dates from the medieval period and reflects the method of cultivation whereby each farmer had strips in a number of different places so that fertile and poor land was shared equally. Enclosure created smaller individually owned fields. This section shows the strips between Miletree Highway, now Vandyke Road, and Hockliffe Highway. Flitch of Bacon Way, which crosses this section of the map, disappeared at enclosure.*

stone and sand from Leighton's heath and using turf cut from the heath as topping each year for their potato pits. The stone was used for mending roads, building walls, sheds and, sometimes, houses.

Despite these appeals all the ancient rights of tenants were swept away by the Enclosure Acts.

98 *(Opposite) The map produced by Benjamin Bevan in 1819. This is the first detailed map of Leighton showing the town before the railway and enclosure. It details the houses clustered around the three main roads which lead out to the open fields surrounding the town. Enclosure allowed people to build farmhouses on their own fields and sell plots of land for development.*

The heath was auctioned off in lots and planted with trees. On more fertile land farms were set up, often creating pastures for dairy herds and sheep on land that was previously farmed in strips for barley, wheat and oats. On these new land holdings Leighton also became a centre for market gardening. The railway provided a rapid means of getting milk and other produce to the lucrative London markets where the demand for fresh food was large and increasing.

The new land holdings and the canal and railway also provided opportunities for new crops. A swathe of land between Stanbridge and Aylesbury, including Billington, where

100 *An area saved at enclosure for continued use as a village green. This Victorian photograph, taken by the Piggotts, of Heath Green shows the clock tower over the pump. The Methodist Chapel is in the background with Irons Row on the left.*

clay overlaid the chalk, allowed the planting of orchards, particularly plums. The Billington plum was particularly prized and used in the dyeing industry. Some were used locally in straw hat manufacturing but larger quantities were sent north in barges for use in the cloth industry. The orchards of all sorts were also used for keeping Aylesbury ducks, which were sent to London markets.

Many new landowners around Leighton found that selling their land in chunks for development of new houses was more lucrative than farming, and enclosure allowed new roads and development on what had been common fields. Many old roads, including the ancient Thiodweg, were stopped up at this time. Another local feature, the Row Riddy Stone, disappeared. This was marked on maps at the point where Leighton's road to Woburn opened out to the heath, but it vanished with Victorian road improvements and is believed to be buried under the embankment in Heath

101 *The limekilns north of Whichello's Wharf on the west of the canal. There are kilns marked all along the canal on early maps, showing the importance of lime for building the new town of Linslade.*

Road which bridges the Row Riddy stream. No one now knows what it looked like.

The only remaining common land from once large areas was at Heath Green, where the clock tower and the well still stand, and part of Reach Green by Bryant's Lane. At Billington and Stanbridge small portions of the greens were allowed to remain as recreation grounds.

The combination of enclosure's impact on changing agriculture and the opportunity for trade opened up by the canal and railway brought new industries to Bedfordshire. As the 1830 directory for the town showed there was already a lime and brick trade, limekilns being built alongside the canal in Linslade to process the chalk brought from the Chilterns. Lime had to be made locally as it was too dangerous to transfer by canal, reacting violently in contact with water.

Bricks were made from the blue gault clay. The principal sites were Grovebury Farm, Hockliffe Road, Plantation Road, Stanbridge Road and Vandyke Road. On the site of one of these brick works on the old Linslade

Road from Heath and Reach, a number of small lakes, now in private gardens, mark the pits where the clay was dug out. The main export from the area was sand, of all grades and types, at least 25 sorts having specialist uses. This rapidly expanding industry led to the opening of new pits and demand for sand carters and sand dobbers, men who lived dangerous lives excavating thousands of tons of material by hand.

Sand was taken by narrowboat both north and south to help build the rapidly expanding West End of London and the Midland industrial towns. However, Leighton's sand had other more specialist uses. The silver or silica sand has always been the most valuable and was used in foundries, where resin coated sand mouldings were used for casting precision machinery. From the earliest days of water companies, it was also used for filtering impurities from tap water. Sand from Leighton is still exported all over the world for this purpose. But perhaps the most prestigious use of the pure Leighton white sand was in glassmaking.

102 *Sand being dug by hand in a Leighton Buzzard pit. The man with the barrow is moving the clay overburden from one side of the pit to the other on a narrow plank bridge. The diggers undermined the sand cliff to cause a collapse. This was highly skilled and dangerous work. Some men were trapped and crushed. A 'mortuary room' at the Red Lion at Reach was set aside for such casualties.*

103 *These men called 'sand dobbers' dug by hand prior to the introduction of mechanised diggers. Narrow gauge railway wagons were used to transport the sand within the pits and eventually a network of lines connected the quarries to the canal and railway.*

Chance Brothers, whose Wolverhampton and Smethwick glass works were next to the Grand Junction Canal, bought their own pit in Miletree Road, Leighton, in order to obtain the best sand. In 1832 Chance Brothers became the first company to adopt the cylinder method of producing sheet glass and became the largest British manufacturer of window, plate and optical glass. The sand to make this glass was transported by horse and cart to a wharf at the Old Linslade canal bridge. Three barges, each with a 30-ton capacity, were loaded at a time. It took five days for the barge horses to pull the load to Smethwick.

Chance Brothers were optical pioneers and made precision optics for lighthouses both in Britain and overseas, but perhaps their most famous work was the glass for the Crystal Palace for the Great Exhibition in 1851 – the only company at the time capable of making so much sheet glass. There is no record of the company's sand coming from anywhere else but Leighton, so it seems likely that the town's pits provided the raw material for some of their other prestige projects. Among them was the glazing of the Houses of Parliament, including the opal glass put together like pieces of a stained glass window for the face of Big Ben in the Westminster clock tower. The ornamental windows in the White House in America were another special project.

The 1830 directory also refers to ironworks. There were two in Leighton, the Gilbert Foundry, which began life as a forge in the

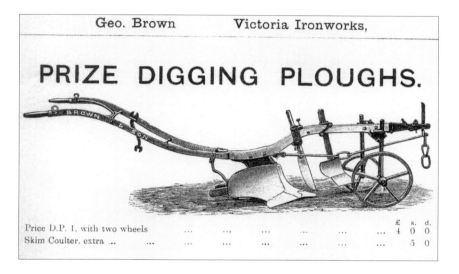

SMITHFIELD CLUB SHOW,
Dec. 10th to Dec. 14th,
AGRICULTURAL HALL, LONDON, N.

GEO. BROWN & SON

Will EXHIBIT on STAND No. 150,

HENSMAN'S PATENT DRILL,

Fitted with NEW LIFTER (patent applied for), and a

COLLECTION OF PRIZE PLOUGHS,

PATENT LEVER HORSE HOES ETC.

An inspection will be esteemed.

VICTORIA IRON WORKS, LEIGHTON BUZZARD.

Geo. Brown   Victoria Ironworks,

PRIZE DIGGING PLOUGHS.

						£	s.	d.
Price D.P. 1, with two wheels	...	...	...	...	...	4	0	0
Skim Coulter, extra ...	...	...	...	...	...		5	0

104-6 *(and* **107** *overleaf) One of Leighton's most successful and long-standing industries is Brown's. George Brown named his Victoria Iron Works in Lake Street after the Queen and was well enough known to exhibit award-winning designs at the Smithfield Club Show in London. The company's commercial expansion was built on its own improved designs for new ploughs, seed drills and water carts, two of which are shown here. Brown's served Leighton's farming community and their machines were sold all over Europe.*

PRICES.

						£	s.	d.
MEDIUM SIZE, to hold 150 Gallons	...	...	...	...	...	15	15	0
LARGE ,, ,, 200 ,,	...	...	...	...	...	16	16	0
IMPROVED SPREADER (Galvanized Iron), extra ...		...	...	...	...	1	5	0

The above Carts are well balanced, and being fitted with wrought Tubular Shafts and Iron Wheels, with chilled renewable bushes, are very durable. Valve with brass fittings, &c.

Leighton Buzzard, England.

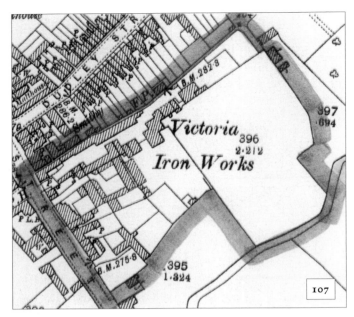

Victorian era only to disappear in the 20th century, Brown's grew as successive generations expanded the business. The Victoria Iron Works in Lake Street was Brown's headquarters and manufacturing base. William, son of the founder George Brown, ensured the success of the business by designing and building efficient agricultural machinery. He started by buying the patents of a seed drill of a rival company, Hensman and Sons of Linslade, which went into liquidation in 1874. The refined design became known as the Bedfordshire drill and was sold all over the British Isles. The company became a major manufacturer of farm implements of all kinds.

yard of *The Peacock Inn* and later moved to Beaudesert, and Brown's, which began as a forge in Lake Street. Unlike many businesses in Leighton that began and prospered in the

109 *The Bethel Baptist Chapel in New Road, Linslade. The Baptists were the first nonconformists to be recorded in Leighton. The dissenting faiths were popular among the working classes and many chapels were built in both towns. This one, built in 1843, was one of the first buildings in New Road and is still in use.*

George Brown, like many prominent Leighton citizens of the time, was both strongly religious and a nonconformist. He worshipped as a Baptist.

The 1830 directory made special mention of the nonconformists – Baptists, Methodists and particularly the Quakers. One family in

108 *(Opposite) The south side of Hockliffe Street, Leighton showing the massive Methodist Chapel with accompanying manses on each side for the ministers. Only the right hand manse remains, renamed Ark House, and now a veterinary surgery. The chapel and the left-hand manse were demolished to make way for the inner ring road.*

particular, the Bassetts, came to be leaders of the community and remained highly influential for more than a century. The Leighton dynasty began with Peter Bassett, who arrived in Leighton around 1773 and became a draper in the town. Like all Quakers, the Bassetts thought the education of their children was paramount, and both boys and girls were sent away to Quaker schools in Hitchin and York. This was not because there were no schools in Leighton, but they were fee-paying Church of England schools and not for everyone. As early as 1655 the vicar of Linslade, Edward Hargrave, was also described as the schoolmaster of Leighton Buzzard, and he remained so for 52 years. He would have taught basic reading, writing and arithmetic to the sons of traders and merchants who could pay modest fees.

Various members of the Leigh family, as lords of the manor, later left money for the education of 10 poor boys so they could read and write, and the Charity Commissioners reported that in 1710 Joshua Pulford, vicar of All Saints, had died and in his will provided for the education of children of the poor. In 1790, when the Hon. Mary Leigh paid for the first purpose-built school in the town in Church Square, now the post office, it was called Pulford School in his honour.

The first floor of the Town Hall, when not being used for manor courts and other meetings, was also in use as a schoolroom. Local artist George Arnald, who painted the Town Hall in 1790, recalls his school days and his teacher, John Young, who was recorded as schoolmaster in 1763. A poem from his diary recalls:

> *Leighton thy market house remembered oft*
> *Where Young the cruel kept his school aloft.*
> *He was a man of whom it might be said*
> *That grace and pity from his heart had fled,*
> *He dealt in words and blows, but what was worse,*
> *His words were few; but his blows came first.*

One form of education for the poor was also a way of exploiting children. At lace

110 *A Piggott photograph dating from the end of the 19th century showing a group of children outside the Mary Bassett School, Bassett Road, Leighton.*

schools children were employed from the age of six to make lace; but even worse were the plait schools, where boys and girls as young as three were made to plait straw for the hat industry. The excuse for this child labour was that rudimentary reading and writing were taught as the children worked, so employers could claim they were a school and not a factory. Older children sometimes worked from 9 a.m. to 9 p.m. to earn two thirds of an adult wage.

The three dissenting faiths, Quakers, Methodists and Baptists, all ran Sunday schools in their chapels to give both children and adults, who were working the rest of the week, a basic education.

In 1813, in order to fill what was perceived as a serious gap in the education needs of the town, the Quakers built what was called a Lancasterian School on the corner of what is now East Street and Beaudesert. The name came from Quaker educationalist David Joseph Lancaster. The school provided education for children and some adult classes. In the first two years 192 boys and 202 girls attended day classes at the school and another 147 boys and 110 girls attended evening tuition.

The school continued to teach boys and girls until 1839, when East Street became boys only and girls and infants were transferred to a new school on Bassett Road. Peter Bassett's son, John Dollin Bassett, who had been sent away to school at Hitchin, was the chief subscriber to the Lancasterian School, along with John Grant, the prominent Quaker businessman with a wharf on the canal. The Bassett family also led the list of subscribers when the new school was built in 1839.

Another Quaker, Theodore Harris, who had married into the Bassett family, established Leighton Buzzard Working Men's Institute on North Street in 1866 with a library and a reading room. Other later institutes offered evening classes as

111 *Part of North Street from the 1901 Ordnance Survey map showing where the town's fire engine was kept at the back of the Wheatsheaf public house. Also shown are the Wilkes Almshouses, the Friends Meeting House with the burial ground behind, the Working Men's Institute and, opposite that, a Primitive Methodist Chapel.*

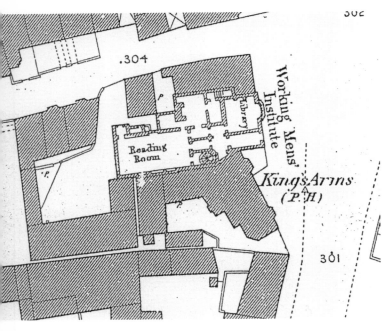

112 *A plan of the Working Men's Institute in North Street. This was built before the town library and in competition with the pubs of the town. Its objectives were 'to afford to the inhabitants of Leighton Buzzard and neighbourhood readily accessible means for social intercourse, mutual help and improvement, and rational recreation, by means of Lectures, Entertainments, Reading Room, Conversation and Smoking Room, Library, Discussions, Classes etc.'*

well, including the Forster Institute built in Linslade. These establishments gave rise to a series of exhibitions, mini versions of the Great Exhibition of 1851, where inventions and marvels of the Victorian Age were displayed for the benefit of the town.

To counteract the increasing influence of nonconformists, the Church of England provided funds for so-called National Schools

in Anglican parishes to teach the Anglican faith as well as reading and writing. The first National School was the one built next to St Barnabas' Church in Linslade in 1849. It was not until the Education Acts of 1870 and 1880 that schooling became compulsory for every child between five and ten.

The fresh air of the country round Linslade was in sharp contrast to the gloomy fumes

113 *The Forster Institute in Waterloo Road, Linslade was built in 1890 by Mrs Charlotte Forster in memory of her husband. She lived nearby in Linslade House, Church Road. The institute was the only meeting hall for the new town.*

114 *St Barnabas' Church, Linslade was built in 1848 as part of the 'new town'. Until then parishioners walked more than a mile to St Mary's Church, Old Linslade.*

115 *(Below) A plan of St Barnabas' Church showing the first National School, Linslade, which opened a year after the church, as shown in the Ordnance Survey large-scale town plan of 1880. The School is now St Barnabas' Church Hall.*

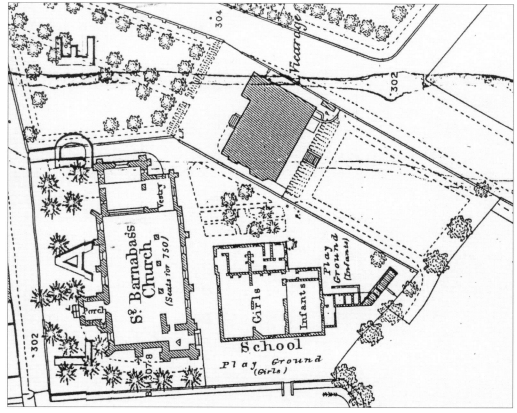

of London and a number of small boarding schools for children of London's middle classes and minor gentry were established in Linslade. They particularly advertised the locality of Leighton as 'beautiful and salubrious', 'amid wild and varied scenery' and 'known to be one of the healthiest in England'. The dryness of the atmosphere attributed to the sand soil was supposed to be particularly healthy. These schools probably also took non-boarders from local families who could afford to pay the fees.

The Quakers had become the town philanthropists but were not always popular in Leighton. Minutes of the Quaker meeting in 1789 recalled windows of shops and furniture being damaged. An explanation is provided by newspapers of the time. There had been national rejoicing at the recovery of George III from madness, but the Quakers thought lighting up their windows would be too excessive a show. Judging by the damage done, the townsfolk reacted badly to their moderation. Another decision by the group of Quaker shopkeepers, not to open on Sundays, the Lord's Day, was not welcomed either. John Grant, particularly, had some difficult times and was accused in his capacity as a dealer in corn of 'sending away large quantities of wheat at night' to keep the price up. In a time of crop failures, bread shortages

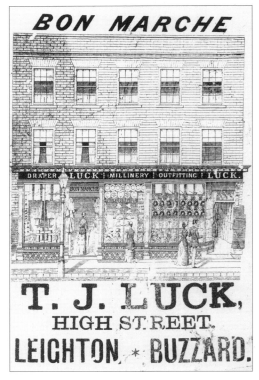

116 *A drawing of the new Bassett's Bank dated 1866. Its design was so notable that it was featured in The Building News of 21 December that year. The bank had eight branches in neighbouring towns.*

117 *A drawing lifted from a paper bag advertising T.J. Luck's 'Bon Marche' store opposite Bassett's Bank in the High Street. This centre of high fashion, including locally made straw hats seen in the window, was run by Thomas James Luck from 1890-1906.*

118 *Public spaces for recreational use were regarded as important in the Victorian era. After enclosure, fenced fields meant the countryside was no longer open and accessible. This field was bought in 1891 by Leighton Urban District Council from the Church Commissioners for use as a park. The Bassett family helped pay for trees to be planted here. On Bevan's map this is named as Parsonage Close and is now known as Parson's Close. The picture shows the park before Church Avenue was built.*

and some famine, he felt obliged to publish a denial of the accusation.

John Dollin Bassett, however, became Leighton's best known and most philanthropic citizen, as well as being an astute businessman. In 1812, along with his father Peter, whose draper's business had prospered, and three other prominent Quakers, he helped to found Leighton's first bank, Bassett, Grant & Co. At first the bank was run from the front room of a house at 38 High Street. One of the tasks entrusted to the fledgling bank was the issue of new silver coins in 1817 to replace existing ones. This had become necessary because of the illegal practice of clipping bits off the old coins, thus debasing the currency.

The bank survived a number of economic upheavals and by 1866 was sufficiently

affluent to employ Alfred Waterhouse, a young architect, to build new premises, now Barclay's Bank in the High Street. Waterhouse, who went on to design such national treasures as the Town Hall in Manchester, The Strand Law Courts in London and the Natural History Museum in Kensington, designed the bank with a reinforced steel shell and steel shutters for the windows. No expense was spared for the interior, with fittings of oak, mahogany and ebony. Above was a spacious home for the manager.

Even before the new bank was built, however, John Dollin Bassett and his family had contributed much to the architecture and appearance of the town. After the enclosure of the heathland north of Leighton, he bought large sections of it and planted trees, many

119 *This rather grand terrace in Church Square replaced a jumble of ancient thatched buildings. The terrace was built by the Bassett family who bought the land for £5,000 in 1852.*

of which remain. He employed the gardener Robert Marnock and within 30 years the plantation had become 'an arboricultural Arcadia, so rich is it with trees from 100 climes'. Even though housing estates have subsequently been built amongst these trees along Plantation Road, many magnificent specimens remain.

His philanthropy and religious conviction also contributed memorable buildings to the town. One of them is the classically styled Temperance Hall in Lake Street, which became the town library before the current modern building opposite replaced it.

In 1852, on the west side of Church Square, John Dollin Bassett bought part of the old prebendal estate that had belonged to the Leigh family and built a terrace of six houses in the Italianate style. To encourage prospective buyers each house was offered for sale with a free first-class railway season ticket to London for 21 years. In 1861 there were 11 'up' trains and 12 'down' trains to London a day. The non-stop fast trains took an hour. The age of the commuter had begun.

Next to this terrace, facing up the High Street, Bassett built himself an eight-bedroom mansion, with two staircases. Gas and hot

120 *The Corn Exchange facing the Unicorn pub in Lake Street. The tower of the Corn Exchange was taken down in the 1932 because it was considered unsafe but the building continued in use as a cinema, dance hall and meeting place until the early 1960s when it was demolished.*

water for the bathroom were laid on. It was designed by the same architect who built the terrace next door, W.C. Read. Subsequently this formed the main building of Leighton's first secondary school, The Cedars, which later became a middle school.

John Dollin Bassett and his son Francis were also prominent in the building of Leighton's Corn Exchange in 1864. This magnificent building was also Italianate in style with a portico of Bath stone, and cost £7,500. The building was built on the boom in corn prices, which collapsed less than 10 years later, forcing the shareholders to put the grandiose building up for auction. John Dollin's son, Francis Bassett, bought the property for £3,100 to ensure that it remained in public use for the town.

Francis, who became the Liberal MP for Bedfordshire for three years from 1872, continued his father's building tradition with his own house. The Heath was built between 1864 and 1869. It was subsequently demolished, but the two lodge houses remain on Plantation Road. Finally, in 1880, he built The Knolls on the other side of Plantation Road, another grand house.

Not that building was confined to the Bassetts. The increase in population of both Leighton and Linslade required new churches. Leighton's population had increased from 1,963 in 1801 to 4,465 by 1851 and Linslade from 203 to 1,309 in the same period. In Linslade, St Barnabas, with adjoining school, was built in 1849 with seating for 750 people. The bells were brought from old St Mary's. In 1867 in Leighton a new church, St Andrew's, was built in the north end of town in what

121 *A remarkable survival of a ticket for a concert at the Corn Exchange during the winter season of 1862. The ticket has survived longer than the building.*

is now St Andrew's Street. Five years later a church school, the first National School in Leighton, was built alongside. Sadly, both were built of local sandstone and weathered badly. A relic of St Andrew's Church is the clock, which has been preserved in the current library in Lake Street, and the lych gate, which still stands.

Across in Linslade a social development of a kind other than philanthropic or religious had been taking place. As well as the industry brought by the railway and canal, the new town had become a fashionable weekend hunting haunt for the gentry. A number of establishments in the new town provided stabling, and grooms stayed in Linslade all week to keep the horses in readiness for the hunting. Part of the attraction was the proximity of the Rothschilds at Ascott House in Wing. For a time Ferdinand de Rothschild lived in Leighton House in the High Street. He bought it in 1880 and lived there while Waddesdon Manor was built, entertaining the beautiful Elizabeth, Empress of Austria, among other nobility.

122 *St Andrew's Church, Leighton Buzzard was built in 1867 from sandstone dug from a neighbouring pit. It closed and was demolished in 1964 because the sandstone had weathered badly and the church was considered unsafe. The site was later used to build Page's Almshouses and St Andrew's Close.*

123 *Leighton House, where Ferdinand de Rothschild lived in the 1880s while Waddesdon Manor in Buckinghamshire was being built. It was a grand house with a library and formal gardens. The Rothschilds' paddock at the rear adjoining Parson's Close is now Church Avenue.*

The *Hunt Hotel*, across the recreation ground from the station, was a centre for the hunting fraternity, 'where peers, members of parliament, cabinet ministers, judges, barristers, authors, actors, soldiers, ex-chancellors ... who have good horses and can ride straight in the Vale (of Aylesbury), elbow one another in passages, at the stables and in the coffee-room', according to the biography of Robert Grimston, fourth son of the Earl of Verulam.

Two heirs to the throne, Albert Edward, Prince of Wales and later Edward VII, and Edward, Prince of Wales, briefly Edward VIII and then Duke of Windsor, hunted locally. The *Leighton Buzzard Observer* for February 1871 describes the Rothschild staghounds, followed by the Prince of Wales, plus various Rothschilds, the Duke of Norfolk, lords and marquises and the Hon. Robert Grimston, chasing a deer through Linslade, down Leighton High Street and along Lake Street towards Billington.

9
War, Peace and War Again

Leighton was lucky that two pioneer photographers, brothers William and Theo Piggott, set up a chemist's shop in the High Street in 1869. For 40 years they recorded many of the town's buildings and people. So well known were they that on 7 February 1905 they were summoned by telegram to Lord Rosebery's home at Mentmore Towers to take a picture of the 'house party', the central figure at the party being King Edward VII. The *Leighton Buzzard Observer* recorded that 'the picture of the King is an excellent one'.

The most famous Piggott photograph of Leighton Buzzard was taken of the market place about 1898, believed to be from scaffolding on the top of the Town Hall. This captures a typical market day at the turn of the century and shows the animals penned in the street for sale.

But many of the photographs the two men took were designed for an entirely different purpose. They came from a family of devout Methodists and made a series of lantern slide shows, each slide depicting an episode of a morality tale. They included stories of runaway children and redemption from the evils of drink. Many of these slides were posed against the backdrop of Leighton buildings.

124 *A rare picture of William Piggott, the older of the two brothers who were partners in the High Street chemists which later became the town's leading photographic studio. He is taking delivery of a tortoise. The label says 'Livestock, With Great Care' and is addressed to W. Piggott, High Street, Leighton Buzzard.*

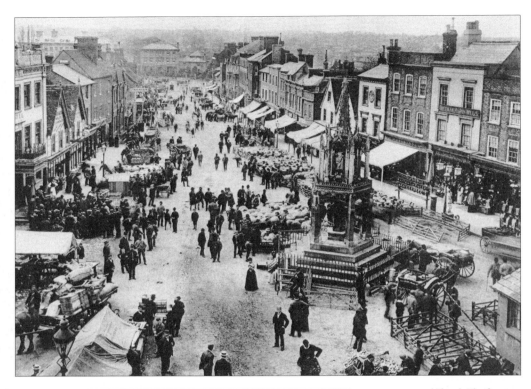

125 (Above) The famous photograph taken by William Piggott about 1898 of Leighton market in full swing. To the right of the Market Cross is a clock above the shop of Matthews, the watch and clock makers. At the far end of the High Street can be seen the Cedars in Church Square, the house built by John Dollin Bassett about forty years before.

126 (Left) A parade on 9 August 1902 in the High Street, Leighton, a joint celebration for the end of the Boer War and the Coronation of Edward VII. The men on horseback are the Bedfordshire Imperial Yeomanry. The street light is lit by gas.

While Leighton still traded as a market town, industry continued to grow in both towns. One of the largest businesses was Morgan and Co., near the bridge across the canal in Linslade, now a supermarket car park. This company had been in the carriage business in London since 1762, but in 1885 amalgamated with a successful Linslade carriage maker, William King, who built a sleek horse-drawn vehicle called the Battlesden

127 *A Piggott photograph, taken for part of their lantern slide shows, of a couple saying goodbye. The imposing gates of the Cedars survived the collections for metal railings made in the Second World War. The Golden Bell pub is in the background. Just before the Cedars became a school Mary Norton, author of* The Borrowers, *lived here with her parents. Her memories of the vast old house inspired her popular children's books.*

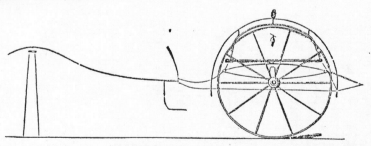

128 *An advertisement for William King, inventor and manufacturer of the 'celebrated Battlesden Car'. The 'steam carriage works' were on the east side of the canal and became Morgans. The main purpose of King's 1877 announcement was to disassociate himself from a rival, George King, who had set himself up in a similar business in Linslade new town.*

car. Among the customers for this vehicle was Lily Langtry, mistress of the Prince of Wales, soon to be Edward VII.

Morgan's, whose slogan was 'built to last', also prospered in Linslade. They maintained showrooms in London but built their carriages locally. As befitted a company at the forefront of fashion, it was natural Morgan's should turn to the manufacture of 'horseless carriages' and as early as 1896 they were building 'two machines on the motor principle'. The size and success of the business can be judged from one of their disasters. A fire in 1901, probably made worse by the quantities of varnish, paint and oil used, devastated their works and between 200 and 300 carriages were lost. Many of them had been prepared for Edward VII's Coronation and the Royal Show at Carlisle.

The combined population of Leighton and Linslade in 1911 was 9,044, reflecting the growth of the town through the creation of industrial jobs. The sand industry, brick works, iron foundries, Morgan's and agricultural machinery manufacturers like Brown's all attracted newcomers, some from as far away as Russia according to the census returns.

But, as with everywhere else in Europe, the twin towns of Leighton and Linslade changed fundamentally in 1914 with the outbreak of the First World War. Many of the district's young men enlisted in the army and the town's industries were turned over to the war effort. The sand quarries, which were already important to the town, became of national significance. Quality Leighton sand was vital for making moulds coated in resin for metal castings. These castings were used in precision engineering throughout the United Kingdom

but in the 1914-18 conflict were needed for making vast quantities of guns and munitions. One of the problems of the industry was the terrible mess the horses and heavy carts made of local roads, transferring the sand from the quarries to the canal and railway, but so important was the sand that the government took over complete responsibility for the repair of roads for the duration of the war.

Many of the local factories were taken over for the war effort. An old building known as the wool store at the bottom of Lake Street was used to make metal rings, clipped together to make vast nets. These were hung on booms on the side of battleships to protect against torpedo attack. A new factory in Grovebury Road was built for the purpose in 1915. Morgan's factory was also turned over to the war effort. Contracts were given to build 250 aircraft used for reconnaissance, training and fighter planes: the De Havilland DH6 was a Royal Flying Corps training aircraft; the curiously named Sopwith one-and-a-half strutter was an early fighter plane; and the Avro 504 was the first aircraft to be used as a bomber in the conflict. In 1917 Morgan's directors were ordered by the government to construct a large building behind their existing works for the building of Vickers Vimy bombers. Forty-two of these enormous planes were built in the war, employing a work force of eight hundred. The finished planes, minus their wings, were wheeled up the High Street and along Lake Street to Billington Road. So tight were the turns that special studs were put in the Market Square and Lake Street for guidance and an apprentice sat in the front gun cockpit to balance the plane. Once in Scott's Field, the

129 *The first Vickers Vimy bomber to be completed at the Morgan Works, which gave its name to the present road into the shopping estate. The Vimy was made by a workforce of eight hundred. Much of the body and wings were made from canvas and linen sewn onto the frame. Seamstresses who worked on the wings can be seen in the front row. Among them is Mrs Violet Kate Guess, whose family still live in Linslade.*

wings, which had followed on behind, were attached and the Royal Flying Corps would take off for the front.

Although bombing of civilian targets was mostly confined to the Second World War, a German Zeppelin raid came close to Leighton on the night of 19 October 1916. It was one of 11 airships that had attempted to bomb the Midlands but got lost. A hooter at Brown's iron works sounded a pre-arranged air-raid warning when the Zeppelin was spotted after a magnesium flare was launched to light up the sky. The Zeppelin was travelling fast, and finding itself over houses in Heath and Reach, dropped 11 bombs. Fortunately they fell harmlessly in fields between Overend Green Farm and Shenley Hill Road. The next day,

souvenir hunters from Leighton found seven craters more than six and a half feet deep and 10 feet wide. The Zeppelin landed in France behind Allied lines and was destroyed by its crew.

Many men who voluntarily enlisted in the army at the start of the war did not return. Later in the war, when the terrible casualty rate became known, there was a series of hearings for people appealing against the draft. The majority lost their appeals.

Most men from Leighton joined the Bedfordshire Regiment, which at full strength had seven battalions totalling 7,000 men. Some joined the Oxfordshire and Buckinghamshire Light Infantry, the regiment favoured by most of the Linslade recruits.

130 *William Holmes, who used the name of his brother in order to enlist at the age of fourteen. He was killed by a shell in 1916. William is wearing the uniform of the Bedfordshire Regiment, with the stag insignia on his collar.*

Of the men who went to the front, 171 from Leighton and 41 from Linslade are listed on the war memorials in Church Square, Leighton, and the Memorial Gardens, Linslade. Only Stanbridge, of all the local villages, has no war memorial, not a single person from the village being killed in either world war.

Records show that most of those who were killed, died in the great battles at the Somme, Ypres and Arras, although some lost their lives at Gallipoli. Some families suffered terrible losses. The three sons of the Going family of Mill Road, Leighton, died in successive years – William, a corporal, in 1916, Francis, a private, in 1917, and Herbert died of wounds in 1918. He was only nineteen.

Robert Richmond, a local magistrate and the author of the first history of Leighton Buzzard,

131 *It took three days to erect Leighton's impressive war memorial in Church Square. It was unveiled two years after the war, on Armistice Day, when over 5,000 people stood in silence.*

132 *When the memorial was unveiled it was already clear that the promise of 'homes fit for heroes' made at the Armistice was not being fulfilled. Lord Ampthill, who led the tributes at the service, said 'the most pitiable sight of all is an ex-soldier begging for his bread'.*

published in 1928, lost two of his three sons, Second Lieutenant Frederick Richmond and Captain Harold Richmond. Both died on the Somme within seven months of each other. A third son, Captain George Richmond, who had been wounded at Gallipoli, went back to fight but survived.

One regular soldier who died was William Holmes, wrongly named as Joseph on a war memorial in France. He had travelled to Dunstable to enlist in the Bedfordshire Regiment at the age of 14 in 1908 and used the name of his older brother, Joseph, to avoid rejection for being too young to serve. He was still known as Joseph by the army when he was killed by a shell on 11 July 1916 and is duly recorded by that name on the battlefield war memorial. His name is correct on the Leighton

memorial in Church Square. His brother, who was a stoker in the Royal Navy, survived. The Holmes family still lives in Leighton.

On the Leighton memorial are listed 12 pairs of brothers, including two sons of Emma Clare of Regent Street who died in the same week in 1917, and one father and his son. About three times as many soldiers were wounded as died and were brought home to recover. Many, whose health had been undermined by gas attacks or the rigours of being in the trenches, died in the 1919 flu

133 *The Linslade war memorial was unveiled on 11 November 1920 on the same day as the one in Leighton. Its original position was in the middle of the road in what was known as Linslade Square, at the junction of the Wing and Old Roads, near the Bedford Arms. The buildings behind it have all been demolished.*

134　(Above, top) A Morgan convertible outside the gates of Mentmore Towers, the home of Lord Rosebery, who married a Rothschild heiress and was Prime Minister. The photograph is from a Morgan brochure of 1924.

135　(Above) Another locally built Morgan from the same brochure. This sporty model was known as the Linslade Coupe. The brochure boasted 'The head folds back particularly neatly so that when down it does not interfere with the passengers in the dickey.'

136　An advert placed by Morgan cars offering one of the many makes of cars they had in stock.

epidemic, which killed as many people in Europe as the war.

Leighton's war memorial was made of the largest piece of granite ever mined in Britain, weighing 22 tons. It had been shipped to London from Shap in Cumbria in 1870 and laid since then, unused, in a London architect's yard. Mr Robert Richmond, the magistrate who lost two sons in the war, located the block of stone and the town bought it. The memorial was unveiled before a crowd of 5,000 on Armistice Day, 11 November 1920.

By this time much had changed in Leighton. The Morgan company had lost its government contract to build planes as soon as the war ended and 500 men were laid off with two weeks pay and the promise of re-employment as soon as the works could be turned around to civilian production. The business was sold the same month, November 1920, for £203,000 to a Mr R.E. Jones, who set about revitalising it.

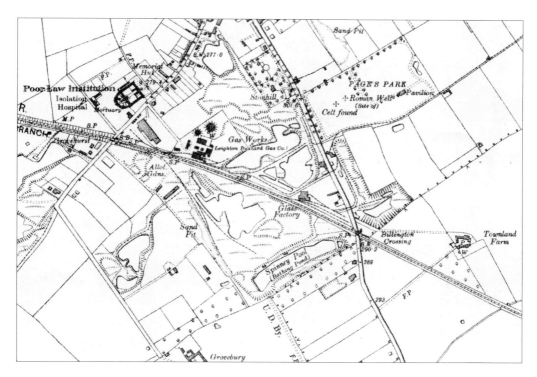

137 *Part of the 1926 six-inch Ordnance Survey map showing the concentration of sand pits south of the town. Crossing the site is the Leighton to Dunstable railway. Also shown are the location of the workhouse, the gas works and the Spinney Pool, a pit converted into a swimming pool. One of the few features remaining unchanged is Page's Park.*

A range of 18 different models were produced and advertised in a lavish brochure of 1924 with testimonials by satisfied customers from as far away as Switzerland. Morgan's were building coachwork on engines and chassis bought from other manufacturers. They also acted as agents for Austin cars and sold the Austin Seven for £149. In the difficult industrial conditions of the 1920s there was not enough demand for the company's luxury cars and the business declined, finally closing in 1930. The premises were taken over by Foundry Equipment, which manufactured complete foundries for installation elsewhere, many being exported. They also produced sand preparation and handling plants and industrial conveyor belts.

The sand industry also had its troubles immediately after the war. Demand was high but the government was no longer prepared to repair the roads and Leighton Town Council refused to allow wagons or steam-driven sand lorries to use them unless the quarry companies paid the repair bills. The two biggest companies, Arnold's and Garside, agreed to solve the problem by building a narrow gauge railway from the pits to the canal and the railway, thereby avoiding the town's roads altogether. Similar railways had been used during the war to take supplies to the front line. The Leighton Buzzard Light Railway was formed in 1919 with a capital of £20,000.

The original plan was for horse-drawn wagons but there were surplus narrow gauge steam engines left over from the war and two unused engines were bought for £1,225 each and delivered to Leighton in time for the opening in 1919. The steam engines were soon replaced by petrol-driven ones and at its height the line served many quarries and carried 100,000 tons of sand a year.

As well as being exported to other parts of Britain and abroad an increasing amount of sand was being used locally. New associated industries included the Marley Tile Company, which began manufacturing in 1928, and the Stonehenge Brick Company in 1935. Both took deliveries from the narrow gauge railway.

A more surprising offshoot of the sand industry was Leighton Buzzard Swimming Club, which was formed in the summer of 1921 when a disused sandpit in Billington Road was acquired as a swimming pool. The clear spring-fed pit known as Spinney Pool was 980 feet long, 160 feet wide and 40 feet deep. Landing stages and changing huts were provided as well as a series of diving boards, the highest 40 feet above the water. The water must have been very cold, but from 1921-39 a swimming gala was held every August Bank Holiday Monday afternoon followed by a dance and carnival, usually attracting more than 100 floats. The Amateur Swimming Association also held many national swimming and diving events at the pool.

One business that grew considerably between the wars was the Leighton Buzzard Laundry. It had been founded in a small way in 1880, but by 1925 employed 150 people, mostly women. The laundry continued

138 *The Spinney Pool was used for recreation for many years and between the wars for national galas. The opening of the Battlesden Pumping Station is said to have caused its closure because the supply from the spring that provided clear water disappeared.*

thriving until the 1970s when the ownership of washing machines and the advent of laundrettes destroyed the business.

The town was blossoming in other ways and in the 1920s had three cinemas. The Grand in Leighton Road, Linslade opened in 1922 as the town's first purpose-built cinema and had 500 seats in balcony and stalls. In the same year a rival, the Oriel, opened in Lake Street having been converted from a house. It seated 800, of whom 326 were in the circle. A third was the Victoria Electric Palace in Hartwell Grove, later called the Old Vic. This was a corrugated iron building which had originally been built as a piano and organ store in 1910. It was Leighton's first cinema, showing two films a week as early as 1912, but it lost business to the better facilities of

139 *Bridge Street between Leighton Buzzard and Linslade, with the Grand cinema on the right pictured soon after it opened in 1922. The cinema advertised a bike shed under lock and key for 'out-of-town patrons'. It was built by Thomas Yirrell, who was also a stonemason; his family still has a butcher's shop in the town.*

the Grand. In the 1930s a dance floor was put in and it became a 'palais de danse' with occasional boxing and wrestling matches and wedding receptions to make ends meet.

The Corn Exchange in Lake Street, which Francis Bassett saved for the town, also showed films during this period, although many other social events and meetings were held there. During the 1920s and '30s the Corn Exchange was also the home venue of a dance band founded by Lawrence Inns. This band became nationally famous and made many radio broadcasts and played background music for films.

140 *The Art Deco Co-op building in Hockliffe Street has a date stone of 1927. At one time the Leighton Co-op sold everything and the large department store took advantage of the new electric light to show off its wares.*

One of the strangest features of the early cinemas was that their projectors worked from batteries which needed recharging at intervals by gas generators to improve the quality of the picture. This was because Leighton and Linslade did not get mains electricity until 1926, almost a century after mains gas had been brought to the town. Pylons were erected

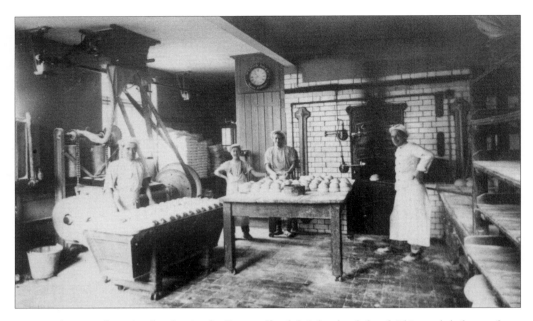

141 *An unusual interior shot showing the Co-op staff and their handmade bread. This was baked every day and sold in a number of the shop's branches in the town.*

to bring 22,000-volt cables from Luton and the pavements were dug up to connect every home that wanted it to the new service. Although there had been private electric generators in the big houses owned by the Bassett family and others since the 1890s, most homes were still lit by gas or lanterns and candles. The new light transformed the lives of many people.

Other advances included a bus service. In the early 1920s what were essentially local services ran two or three times a week round local villages to bring people into town for market days. A garage and coach station was subsequently opened in North Street and long-distance services to Luton and Dunstable began in 1928.

Two tragedies of national significance touched Leighton and Linslade in 1930 and 1931. The first was the last flight of the giant airship, the R101, from Cardington near

Bedford, which passed over Leighton on 4 October 1930 en route for India. It crashed 40 miles north of Paris at 2.30 a.m. the next morning with the loss of 46 lives; only eight of the passengers survived. A special train carrying the dead passed through Leighton on the way to Bedford and a large crowd gathered to pay their respects as the bells of All Saints Church rang for 55 minutes in a muffled peal.

The following year, on 22 March 1931, another disaster occurred when the *Royal Scot* train travelling from Euston to Glasgow crashed at Sunday lunchtime at Leighton Station. The line was being repaired and the train should have diverted from the fast to the slow line. The driver had failed to slow down at a signal and the engine and first five carriages jumped the track and turned on their side, killing the driver, fireman and four passengers. Five others were seriously injured.

142 *Some of the evacuee children arriving at Leighton Buzzard station in 1939. Many stayed in Leighton and the surrounding villages for the entire war. Another group of evacuees, the Chelsea Pensioners, were billeted at Ascott House, Wing, for the duration.*

The outbreak of the Second World War brought dramatic changes to Leighton. Young men again flocked to enlist, this time to a large variety of regiments and different armed services. Some, members of the Dunstable Artillery Territorial Unit, among others, joined up at the outbreak of war and were captured at the fall of Singapore in February 1942, thereby spending the rest of the war as prisoners of the Japanese. Another 52 names were added to the Leighton war memorial and 20 to Linslade's as a result of the conflict. Although relatively close to London, Leighton was seen as a safe haven both for evacuees and businesses vital to the war effort, as well as a hideaway for new top-secret wireless and radar headquarters. The evacuees mostly came by train, some with their mothers. In total 3,100 were allocated to the district and taken to reception centres in public halls and churches, then given a meal while 25 billeting officers allocated them to families.

There was some reluctance in Leighton to take children because several hundred came from the Waifs and Strays Society. Most were from London but some arrived from the industrial areas of the Midlands and Scotland. In October 1939 a second wave of children arrived by bus via a circuitous

143 *A post-war Gossard's advertisement for workers at their Leighton Buzzard factory in Grovebury Road. The company had been making foundation garments in Leighton since 1926 and its sewing skills were enlisted for the war effort in 1939.*

WORK WITH GOSSARD

TOP NAME IN FOUNDATION GARMENTS

Gossard's factory at Leighton Buzzard has been established for 35 years, and its high reputation is reflected in the work produced there. Women and girls who make the glamorous range of bras, panties and girdles take a special pride in their work. This is a job you'll really enjoy. There are pleasant surroundings to work in and a first-class canteen. Why not call in and we will give you further details.

Gossard

GOSSARD LTD
Grovebury Road
Leighton Buzzard

RGA-27

144 (Right) A barrage balloon being checked for holes at Gossard during the Second World War. These photographs were published by the Ministry for War as part of a propaganda campaign to underpin the civilian war effort.

145 (Left) Young Leighton women working inside a barrage balloon in Grovebury Road. The location of the factory was kept secret since these balloons were vital to the defence of Britain's cities against air raids in the Second World War.

route through Rutland. These were 266 boys from the William Ellis School in London who were supposed to share Cedars School, Leighton's only comparable secondary school. So inhospitable was Cedars School to start with that critical articles appeared in the national press about 'the snob school' which had forced newcomers to have their school assembly in Parson's Close, with the headmaster in the bandstand and the pupils

146 A dinghy, also made at Gossard, being checked for seaworthiness. These tiny craft were carried by aircraft and saved the lives of many airmen forced to ditch in the sea after bombing raids or protecting convoys in the Atlantic.

standing in the open air. The Baptists in Leighton offered help and accommodation and a plaque commemorating the school's time in Leighton is on the wall of the Baptist Church schoolroom in Hockliffe Street. Some boys subsequently married Leighton girls and came back to live in the district.

As happened in the First World War, much of the manufacturing plant was turned over to the war effort. The Foundry Equipment Co. made casings for depth charges and other munitions. More spectacular was the work of Gossard, makers of foundation garments, which had set up in Leighton in 1926. In 1939 the company was pressed into service making barrage balloons, dinghies for airmen who ditched in the sea, and parachutes. Particularly important were small parachutes for very light flares. Another firm, Coty's, which made cosmetics, was re-located to Leighton to make the flares, taking over buildings at the Southcott Stud and the old Grand cinema. Local people were employed there making the

147 *Members of the RAF stationed during the war at the secret base of Oxendon House in Plantation Road on their way to a special service on a Sunday morning. Britain's pioneer radar stations were planned and run from this rambling house, which burned down after the war in a spectacular fire.*

148 *The cover of a* Radar *journal, published after the war, which gave details for the first time of the secret work carried out at Oxendon House.*

was the headquarters of the RAF 60 group, responsible for the planning, building, staffing and operation of all the radar stations in Britain during the war. It was called the 'brains and eyes' of the air force, organising our defence in the Battle of Britain and then the bombing raids later in the war. The workhouse in Grovebury Road was requisitioned to house personnel and many were billeted in the town and temporary huts. Many of these huts were made in Leighton by Harbrow Ltd, a London company that had moved its stocks of timber from London docks to Leighton to avoid the blitz.

The decision to hide sensitive industries and evacuees in Leighton and Linslade proved the correct one, the district being almost free of enemy attack. The village of Eggington was bombed on 26 September 1940 at 3 a.m. and the windows of a house were blown in on the Leighton Road but there were no casualties.

There was an enemy attack in Leighton itself in 1943 when a 500 pound bomb exploded near the workhouse in Grovebury Road and incendiary bombs damaged a furniture shop in North Street but, again, no one was hurt.

As well as working in war industries, the whole population contributed to the war effort in other ways. Collections of aluminium pans were made and metal railings were sawn off for

chemicals and folding the parachutes. Among the workforce was Yvonne Rothschild who lived at Ascott House, Wing.

In addition to moving refugees and industry to Leighton, the government set up a top secret underground wireless station in Stanbridge Road and took over Oxendon House, a Victorian lodge in Plantation Road. This

149 *'The Buzzard' Spitfire was paid for by public subscription in 1941 as part of the war effort. Some of the money was raised by charging people to look at the wreckage of a German Messerschmitt on show in the grounds of Cedars School. A giant barometer in Church Square showed how much money was raised each week by the 'Wings for Victory' campaign.*

150 *A street party on 8 May 1945 to celebrate Victory in Europe Day. It was held in Linslade for the children of Rock Lane, Springfield Road and Leopold Road. Another set of parties took place three months later on VJ day, when Japan surrendered after the dropping of two nuclear bombs by the Americans.*

making aircraft and armaments. Enough money was collected in Leighton Buzzard, Linslade and Wing to present the 'Buzzard' Spitfire to the Ministry of Aircraft Production in 1941. The aircraft fought with 19 Squadron of Fighter Command and survived the war to be scrapped in 1945.

In 1942 the area also contributed £160,000 in loans and gifts to the construction costs of the £400,000 destroyer HMS *Oakley*. She had a distinguished career and served in the Arctic and North Sea and the Sicily and South of France landings. Bizarrely, she was sold off to the Federal German Navy as a training ship in 1958.

151 *An Order of Service for a thanksgiving service at St Barnabas' Church, Linslade to mark the end of the Second World War.*

A
SERVICE of THANKSGIVING
for use at the cessation of

hostilities in Europe

PARISH OF LINSLADE

10

Losses and Growing Pains

At the end of the Second World War Leighton and Linslade were still relatively small towns with most residents employed locally. Many of the industries that had grown with the arrival of the canal and the railway in the early 19th century still survived, yet the population in 1951 for Leighton and Linslade combined was only 12,295 people. Twenty years later, in 1971, it had grown dramatically to 20,347. And in the following 10 years, after more large housing estates were tacked onto the green edges of both towns, another 10,000 people arrived.

As these new houses were being built the town's character was changing. Although local industry still flourished, the canal, which 150 years before had transformed Linslade and opened up trade, was rapidly losing business. The families who lived on barges were struggling to find enough cargoes to earn a living. The staples of their trade, sand and coal, were moving to lorry transport. By the mid-1960s Leighton Buzzard was boasting it had more heavy lorries per head of population than any other town in the country. Road haulage was big business in

152 *Many families lived their entire lives on barges, acquiring their own traditions and style of dress. Here a boat family show off their finery during a family christening in 1913. The boat belongs to Faulkners of Leighton Buzzard, a family which built and owned a fleet of 50 boats and had many local families living on them. By the 1950s the commercial traffic had almost disappeared and the vessels were sold for conversion into houseboats.*

153 (*Above*) *Two barges that have just passed under the town bridge heading north. In the background is Whichello's Wharf, now a small housing estate. Also in the picture is an icebreaker built in order to keep the canal open all winter.*

154 (*Left*) *The Railway Inn in the 1980s, before a disastrous fire wrecked the hotel. This was one of the many businesses that benefited before the Second World War from the arrival of the railway and the weekend visitors who came for the hunting.*

Leighton with a number of firms operating across Europe.

The railway, too, was suffering although not as badly. More people were commuting to London but daytime passenger numbers were down and rail freight transport from local firms had almost disappeared. As a result the Leighton-Dunstable branch line was closed in 1962 as part of the national programme recommended by Lord Beeching.

Social conditions were changing, too. The last of the Bassett dynasty, Mary Bassett, who had continued in the philanthropic tradition of the family, died in 1948 at the age of ninety-five. She had founded in the 1890s the Leighton Buzzard Handicraft Class for

Cripples which became world famous and made pieces for Queen Victoria's Jubilee. The Mary Bassett school was named in her honour, but the family's name was otherwise largely forgotten. The legacy of the Bassetts remains in some of the town's more interesting buildings, although others have been lost. In the 1960s the Working Men's Institute in North Street was demolished to become a car park and the Corn Exchange in Lake Street was taken down as unsafe. The Heath on Plantation Road was also demolished to make way for smaller houses.

Other family homes and enterprises were saved. The Cedars remains as a school, the Italianate-style houses in Church Square are now offices and flats, and The Knolls was converted into an old people's home. The family bank's headquarters in the High Street, which had eight branches in 1896 when it amalgamated with another Quaker bank, Barclays, still serves it original purpose. The attractive Temperance Hall in Lake Street has had a series of other uses.

No other family name was as influential in the town's affairs but others have left interesting legacies that are still important. In earlier generations it was the Wilkes family, who built the almshouses in North Street in 1630. These homes were rebuilt in 1873 and still house 12 'poor widows'. The first benefactor, Edward Wilkes, had a wealthy son, Matthew,

who provided for perambulations on Rogation Sunday. This included a reading of his father's will while standing a choirboy on his head to 'concentrate his mind'. (In modern times this might also be a girl chorister.) In the Victorian era the celebration involved cakes and ale distributed outside the *Swan* for every Leighton schoolboy. This caused some disorder, as people fought for the traditional spiced rolls, so the ceremony became more restricted in the 1890s but it still includes an annual will reading outside the almshouses and an upside-down choirboy. In 1903 six new almshouses were built in Church Street using a bequest in the will of Councillor William Sharp Page, a pawnbroker who was also a town councillor. He gave Leighton one of its best open spaces, Page's Park, then a field on the edge of town

Another house that was lost after 1945 was Holly Lodge, a handsome gabled Jacobean house in North Street. Built in 1607, it

155 *The rear of Leighton House seen from the gardens. It was demolished in 1958 to make way for a Co-op store.*

housed evacuees during the war only to be pulled down in 1958 to make way for West Street, a road designed to reduce congestion in the High Street. It cut across the long thin burgage plots laid out behind the shops in the High Street in the 14th century so the owners could have room for workshops and wagons behind. On part of the land next to West Street a new Bossard shopping centre was built, later renamed Waterborne Walk. It was aimed at regenerating the town centre. Leighton House in the High Street, owned by the Rothschilds until 1919, was pulled down in the same year, this time to build a Cooperative Store. Its origins went back to at least the 16th century.

A house in Lake Street that had been home of John Salusbury, Leighton's 18th-century diarist, was also lost. It was the *Maidenhead Inn* before Salusbury made it a private house and survived long enough to be requisitioned by the army in the Second World War. It was knocked down in 1956 to make way for a telephone exchange.

Grand private homes were not the only losses. A building that dominated part of the town was the water tower built in 1896 at the top of the hill on Stanbridge Road. A well 200 feet deep supplied two tanks in the top of the tower and provided a free water supply for the town. It was declared redundant and demolished in the 1950s. Another industrial landmark, the gasworks in Grovebury Road, open since the 1880s, was closed and demolished soon after gas was piped from Reading in 1960.

Linslade had its losses, too. Perhaps the most interesting was the exotic canal-side house, The

156   *The Baptist Chapel in Lake Street during demolition, showing the rose window at the rear. The building was replaced by a housing development called Chapel Mews.*

declared bankrupt. His house was turned into flats and deliberately burned down in 1971.

Some of Linslade's hunting heritage remains, including the *Hunt Hotel* and former hunting lodges Buxton House and Rochester House, but only the billiard room remains of another grand house, The Gables off Wing Road. This house was built for Henry Finch, a wealthy businessman and Linslade benefactor, in the 1880s. He paid for the restoration of St Mary's at Old Linslade in 1897 and bought the fields between the *Hunt Hotel* and the railway station to prevent them from being built on. He gave them to the town as a recreation ground. His house was turned into a girls' school but the main building was lost when the school closed in 1969. The wing containing the billiard room was incorporated into a Masonic Hall built on the site.

157 *The water tower built in 1896 to provide free drinking water supply to the town. It was declared redundant and demolished in the 1950s.*

Martins, built at the turn of the 19th century in the Chinese style for Gordon Cale Thomas, the engineer to the Grand Junction Canal. Among other features it had a tennis court sunk below ground level so it could double as a skating rink in the winter. On 16 May 1916 Thomas was charged with embezzlement at Bow Street Magistrates Court and was subsequently

158 *The Martins was built in the Chinese style in about 1903 by the Grand Union Canal engineer Gordon Cale Thomas. It was an exotic black and white house. The seven bedrooms had balconies overlook the canal and Ouzel Valley. This is now a housing estate but the icehouse and a folly with decorative stone dolphin survive in the grounds of the lodge, which is now a private house.*

One of the most important post-war developments was the amalgamation in 1965 of the two towns of Leighton Buzzard and Linslade to form a new urban district. This had been talked about for years, but many resisted changing the 1,000-year-old boundaries of both town and Beds/Bucks counties along the River Ouzel. The Boundary Commission disagreed and decided that as well as joining the two towns, all of Linslade civic parish should be brought into Bedfordshire, arguing that the two towns were better administered and planned as one and services could be provided for both of them. The headquarters of this new local authority was the White House, the town's distinguished Italianate-style building in Hockliffe Street, which had been bought by the urban district council in 1962. Linslade residents resented the loss of their status as a separate town and town nameplates showing the old boundaries were subsequently reinstated. The final stage in unifying the two towns took place in 2008 when the ecclesiastical parish of Linslade was transferred from the Diocese of Oxford to the Diocese of St Albans, so joining the parishes of All Saints, Heath and Reach, Billington, Eggington and Hockliffe as part of the Ouzel Team Ministry.

Two unrelated events brought Linslade to national attention. The first was the Linslade Tornado of 1951 which entered the record books because it caused the longest track of damage of any tornado in Europe. It started as a water spout, sucking up the contents of the canal at Wendover in Buckinghamshire and finally left the coast at Blakeney in Norfolk. The 100 mile trail of destruction began at 4 p.m. on 21 May 1950 and left the coast at 8 p.m. The storm was named the Linslade Tornado because it caused more damage in the town than anywhere else, particularly in New Road and Old Road where roofs were ripped off. The Ministry of Supply provided 450 roof tarpaulins.

The second event was the Great Train Robbery on 8 August 1963, when the Royal Mail train was stopped by thieves who changed

159-60 (Opposite) A national appeal was made to help the victims of the Linslade Tornado, who had the roofs ripped off their houses on 21 May 1950. Worst affected were New Road and Old Road. Firemen used their turntable ladders to place tarpaulins on houses in New Road, and the next day workmen began to repair the roof of St Mary's Lodge, 43 New Road.

161 Most of Leighton's High Street shops survived the rash of demolitions of the 1950s, and the town celebrated the Coronation of their young Queen on 2 June 1953 by decorating the shops, handing out flags, holding street parties for people of all ages and extending hours in the pubs. Griffin Bros. Electrical was typical of the small independent shops in the High Street at that time.

the green light to red at a lonely but convenient bridge two miles south of Leighton Buzzard station. They smashed their way into a carriage containing 120 mail bags with £2,650,000 in used Bank of England notes. Despite the fact that a railwayman was brutally beaten, the robbery captured the public's imagination because the unmarked notes were on their way to the incinerator and nobody, apart from the Bank of England, was thought to have lost by the theft. It was also the newspaper 'silly season' and the story ran for weeks, partly because stashes of half-buried notes were found in woodland in the south-east of England and so a national treasure hunt began. Much of the money was never recovered. Over many weeks a number of robbers were hunted down and brought to Linslade's tiny magistrates court in Wing Road, which was besieged by the national press. When the defendants went on trial in Aylesbury the courts were anxious to stamp on any romantic notion about the theft and handed down sentences of 30 years for many of the robbers, the longest jail terms ever given by a British court.

Although many of the newcomers to the town travelled to work in London and neighbouring places like Dunstable and Luton, the town retained some of its character. Until the late 1970s the cattle market and associated weekly auction on 'Tiddly Tuesday' was

an important part of town life, the pubs remaining open all day. Local industries also continued to thrive. Sand quarrying, as well as continuing to supply all grades for water filtering and other specialist uses, successfully fed tile and brick manufacturers. The Marley Tile Company employed 350 people and the Leighton Buzzard Tile Company, which was taken over by the Redland group, another 150 workers. In addition, each morning slow-moving heavy lorries left the town loaded with sand for all parts of Britain.

Of the older businesses, Gossard had switched back to manufacturing girdles and in the 1960s produced the 'Wonderbra', which became world famous. The company employed 200 people at its Grovebury Road factory.

Newcomers included Camden Motors, a company that sold new and second-hand

162   *The Scout Hut in Grovebury Road, Leighton, the home of one of the first scout groups in Britain. It is built of Stonehenge Bricks, which were made from Leighton's pale sand at a plant outside the town along Mile Tree Road. They were called 'Stonehenge' because the bricks were supposed to last a thousand years.*

163   *A Linslade-produced Paramount car, with Bill Hudson, the designer, in the driving seat and three colleagues. This was a publicity shot taken on the banks of the canal at Charity Wharf where the cars were made.*

£1,000 meant they could not compete with the cheaper mass-produced models. In total only 85 cars were built.

Two other companies that grew large and prospered were Lancer Boss and Lipton's Tea. Lancer Boss made fork-lift trucks and became the largest manufacturer of this kind of equipment in the UK, exporting all over the world. The company, run by brothers Neville and Trevor Bowman-Shaw, employed more than 800 people and in the 1980s tried to expand its factories into the water meadows behind All Saints Church. A bitter battle with the Leighton Preservation Society ensued. The society set up as a watch-dog on planning matters objected to the flood plain being used and the damage to the historic setting a new factory would cause. The inquiry delayed matters so long that Lancer Boss could no longer carry out the plan and the company was taken over in 1994 by a German rival, which immediately scrapped the proposed expansion.

cars. It began in a small way in Linslade, moved to Charity Wharf and then to Lake Street, where people came from all over the south of England to look at the hundreds of used cars on offer. One offshoot of Camden Motors at Charity Wharf was the manufacture of Paramount Cars. These hand-made four-seater tourers were an attractive design, but the fact they were priced at

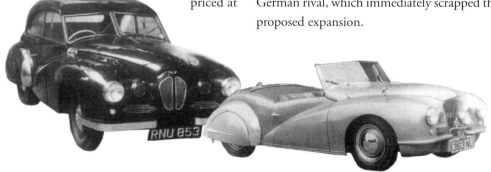

164   *Paramount cars were built in sheds on Charity Wharf on Wing Road, Linslade but these hand-built models shown in the company's glossy brochure could not compete with the mass-produced competition and the company went out of business.*

A new and more powerful

PARAMOUNT

—*Now even more exciting
with the new 1½-litre engine.*

Graceful styling
With ample space for four and their luggage
Aluminium coach-built body
Real leather upholstery
Range of sparkling colours
Full all-weather equipment
Toughened glass windows and quarter lights
Tubular steel chassis
Immensely strong and rigid
New 4-cylinder O.H.V. engine
Now 47 B.H.P.
Remote Control gear lever

PRICE: £675 (Plus P.T. £338.17s.)

PARAMOUNT

Full information and brochures from :

Camden Motors Ltd

LAKE STREET, LEIGHTON BUZZARD, BEDS.   Tel. : 2041 (5 lines)

165   *The Paramount cars took pride of place in Camden Motors showrooms in Lake Street, Leighton, as this 1956 advertisement in* Autocar *shows. There are believed to be 15 of these cars still in existence, restored by enthusiasts.*

Lipton's, manufacturers of tea bags for export, moved to Leighton in 1974 and was extremely successful. The company employed more than 700 people before closing down completely after 25 years and moving to the Middle East to take advantage of cheaper labour.

Many smaller companies, both independent and branches of larger manufacturers, continue to thrive in Leighton, particularly along the Grovebury Road, where the original workhouse now provides modern office accommodation. Other areas of the town, the site of Camden Motors and some of the disused haulage yards, have been turned into housing estates. Others, like the Morgan Carriage Works, were demolished and replaced by giant supermarkets, the town centre suffering a decline as a result.

Some of the industrial infrastructure which once brought jobs and prosperity to Leighton Buzzard has been reborn as a visitor attraction. The narrow gauge railway, which had come into being to save Leighton's roads from destruction, gradually fell into disuse as lorries became a cheaper form of transport. A group of enthusiasts formed the Leighton Buzzard Light Railway and in 1967 took over the line with encouragement from the sand company, Arnold's, which by then was the sole owner and operator. It is now one of the town's main tourist destinations and operates trips for families and enthusiasts.

The canal has also been rejuvenated as a place for walking, cycling and boating, with a thriving canoe club and annual waterside festival. One company that converted itself from a coal carrier into a boating holiday specialist is the Wyvern Shipping company, based in Rothschild Road, Linslade. In its canal-side dry dock the company builds and equips its own narrow boats for canal holidays and runs more than 30 for hire.

The town's best known and most spectacular building remains All Saints Church. The spire is 13th-century and the interior has an 'angel roof' added in the 15th century. These highly painted angels appear to be holding up the ends of the roof beams. Following a full restoration in 1985 an extensive fire destroyed much of the roof of the nave and chancel. It also caused serious structural damage to the spire, tower and vestry. The 12 bells were lost, as was the church clock and two organs. The total cost of the damage exceeded £2 million. Despite the shock and the dangerous state of much of the church the congregation started work on restoration the next day and All Saints has again been superbly restored to its original condition.

As this history of the towns of Leighton and Linslade was being written a new chapter was beginning in the shape of another local government reorganisation and plans for an even greater expansion of housing development. In 1974, nine years after Linslade was brought into Bedfordshire and joined with Leighton, the new urban district council formed to run the two towns was abolished and was replaced by a new town council and a much larger South Bedfordshire District Council. This had most of

166 *Wyvern Shipping in Rothschild Road, which hires out holiday cruisers and keeps Leighton's boat-building tradition alive. The family-owned business buys steel hulls and builds and fits out its own narrowboats for holiday cruising in a canal-side dry dock.*

167 *Leighton's narrow gauge railway has become a draw for the nation's steam train enthusiasts and families on a day out. A large number of locomotives, which would otherwise have been scrapped, have been lovingly restored and are in regular use pulling passengers through the town.*

the powers of the old urban district council and, most importantly, controlled planning. The new administration brought Leighton, Linslade, Dunstable and Houghton Regis together.

Over the next 20 years the population of Leighton and Linslade continued to expand as new estates were built on farm land in Linslade, on the sites of old sandpits in Leighton, and on most of the land which had once been the airfield at RAF Stanbridge. A southern bypass was opened in 1991 and in 2007 a dual carriageway forming the Linslade and Stoke Hammond bypass was added. Despite these roads, the traffic in Leighton town centre was still often at a standstill.

Putting the four towns together under a new council resulted in the headquarters and power base moving from Leighton to Dunstable. With it went most of the council jobs and many of the amenities of the district. Dunstable has seen the building of a new £12 million theatre while Leighton, a town slightly larger in size, had no money spent on any similar venture at all. In 2007 Leighton's Old Town Hall and market were privatised.

The town's population is set to top 40,000 and thousands more houses are being planned on greenbelt land amid objections from existing residents. Protestors claim that the town has barely enough facilities to support its existing population, there are not enough job prospects in the locality, and public transport is inadequate. New residents would need cars to reach both work and shops and be forced to use a road structure which is already overloaded.

In April 2009 a new council covering an even larger area, including mid-Bedfordshire, will take over from South Bedfordshire District Council. Meanwhile, in Leighton Buzzard a new organisation has been set up to revitalise the historic town centre. The long history of Leighton Buzzard and Linslade continues to unfold.

BIBLIOGRAPHY

Alexander, Bruce, *Before Domesday: Haddenham & Cuddington*, Thame (2008)

Baines, Arnold H.J., *The Lady Elgiva, St Aethelwold and the Linslade Charter of 966*, Records of Bucks., Vol. XXV, Aylesbury (1983)

Baker, Evelyn, *La Grava: The Archaeology and History of a Royal Manor and Alien Priory of Fontevrault*, forthcoming (2009)

Beckett, Constance M., *The Sky Sweepers*, London (1995)

Bell, Patricia, *Aspects of the History of Leighton and Linslade*, Bedford (1986)

Branigan, Keith, *The Catuvellauni*, Gloucester (1983)

Brown, Maureen, *Leighton Linslade Heritage Exhibition Souvenir Brochure*, Leighton Buzzard (1986)

Brown, Maureen and Masters, June, *Around Leighton Buzzard & Linslade*, Stroud (1998)

Brown, Maureen and Masters, June, *The Bassetts: Leighton Buzzard's First Family*, Leighton Buzzard (1989)

Brown, Maureen, Masters, June and Lawson, Tom, *The Old Pubs of Leighton Buzzard & Linslade*, Leighton Buzzard (1994)

Calder, Guinevere E., *The History of Eggington*, Luton (1986)

Dingwall, Rod, *Narrow Gauge Tracks in the Sand: The Leighton Buzzard Light Railway*, Oxford (1997)

Gelling, Margaret, *The Early Charters of the Thames Valley*, Leicester (1979)

Godber, Joyce, *History of Bedfordshire*, Bedford (1969)

Gurney, Frederick G., *Yttingaford and the C10th Bounds of Chalgrave and Linslade*, Bedfordshire Historical Record Society, Vol. 5, Part 2, Bedford (1920)

Hart, Richard, *Pictures Past and Present*, Luton (1986)

Hassell, J., *Tour of the Grand Junction Canal* (1819)

Hyslop, Miranda, *Two Anglo-Saxon Cemeteries at Chamberlains Barn, Leighton Buzzard*, The Royal Archaeological Institute, The Archaeological Journal, Vol. 120, London (1964)

Jones, J. Bernard, 'An Archaeological Assessment of the Ancient Parishes of Leighton Buzzard and Linslade', thesis, Oxford (1997)

Lawson, Tom, *Leighton Buzzard Then & Now*, Leighton Buzzard (1992)

Lawson, Tom, *Then and Now Leighton Buzzard and Linslade*, Vol. 2, Leighton Buzzard (1992)

Leighton and Linslade Town Guides, 1962-98

Leighton Buzzard and District Archaeological and Historical Society, Transactions I (2007), Transactions II (2008)

Matthews, C.L. and Schneider J.P., *Ancient Dunstable*, Dunstable (1989)

Moore R. et al., *A4146 Stoke Hammond and Linslade Western Bypass Archaeological Excavations 2005*, Records of Bucks., Vol. 47, Part 1, Aylesbury (2007)

Morley, Ken and Margaret, *'Tis The Far Famous Vale. National Influences on the Vale of Aylesbury*, Dunstable (2007)

Morris, John, *Domesday Book Bedfordshire*, Chichester (1977)

Morris, John, *Domesday Book Buckinghamshire*, Chichester (1978)

Pigot and Co.'s National Commercial Directories 1830: Bedfordshire and Buckinghamshire, facsimile editions, Kings Lynn (1992, 1994)

Reed, Michael, *A History of Buckinghamshire*, Chichester (1993)

Richards, Peter and Simpson, Bill, *A History of the London & Birmingham Railway Vol. I Euston to Bletchley*, Witney (2004)

Richardson, John, *The Local Historian's Encyclopedia*, New Barnet (1974)

Richmond, Robert, *Leighton Buzzard and its Hamlets*, Leighton Buzzard (1928)

Rutherford Davis, K., *Britons and Saxons The Chiltern Region 400-700*, Chichester (1982)

Simco, Angela and McKeague, Peter, *Bridges of Bedfordshire*, Bedford (1997)

Stannard, Maggi, *The Town Hall in Leighton Buzzard*, Leighton Buzzard (2004)

Stannard, Maggi, *The Way to School*, Leighton Buzzard (1990)

Swanton, Michael, *The Anglo-Saxon Chronicle*, London (1996)

Stephenson, Joseph, *William of Malmesbury, The Kings Before the Norman Conquest*, Llanerch (1989)

Warburton, Terry, *Through Fire and Rebirth, All Saints Church*, Leighton Buzzard (1992)

Willis, R.V., *The Coming of a Town*, Luton (1984)

Wilson, Ian J., *The Grand Union Canal from Brentford to Braunston*, Stroud (2004)

Index

Numbers in **bold** refer to illustrations.

Ordnance Survey 1926 map of Leighton and Linslade showing how undeveloped the two towns still are before the Second World War.